THE COMPLETE GUIDE TO
SUCCESSFUL BUSINESS NEGOTIATION

The Complete Guide to
Successful Business Negotiation

By K. H. Nothdurft

LEVIATHAN HOUSE
LONDON & NEW YORK

FIRST PUBLISHED IN ENGLISH, JANUARY 1974

© Verlag Moderne Industrie 1972

ISBN 0 900537 16 7

Library of Congress Catalog Card No. 73-77706

PRINTED IN GREAT BRITAIN BY
BILLING AND SONS LIMITED, GUILDFORD AND LONDON

Contents

PART TWO: THE STRUCTURE OF A
              DISCUSSION

PART FOUR: SOME TYPICAL DISCUSSIONS

A*

Introduction

"The purpose of having discussions is to exchange ideas." That is one view. "The aim of talks is to make one's own ideas prevail in spite of other peoples' objections." That is a slightly different attitude.

Should one ask here who is right and who is wrong? I don't think so. Why should we always start with a definition? Having discussions is not an end in itself, but rather a means to an end. Here we shall be seeing how these means are most effectively employed.

Recently someone said to me: "Why should I concern myself with how to hold a conversation? After all, nature has seen fit to provide me with organs of speech, I have inherited a certain amount of common sense from my parents, I have learnt the principles of grammar at school, and I draw my vocabulary from the press, radio and television. All I need to do is to combine these four elements skilfully together, extend my lower jaw a little and off I go." This is in fact how the majority of conversations are conducted today, both in the social and, regrettably, in the commercial sphere.

Take a look at delegates at business conferences who have just sat through their obligatory three to four hours, or have a word with them sometimes. Have a talk with your colleague on his way back from a "consultation" with the boss. Consider how frequently people return dissatisfied, annoyed or even angry from such "discussions".

Today we can learn and study all manner of specialised subjects; we receive certificates, diplomas, degrees. Yet whenever it is necessary for us to apply, communicate or make intelligible this specialised knowledge to others, we find we lack the simplest of expedients: how to speak to the other person.

Moreover, conversations are not merely a tiresome by-product of work, but are themselves a form of work. One must work with and also within the conversation. Anyone who regards conversations as a necessary evil, a waste of time and a wearisome diversion from preoccupation with oneself, will never be able to conduct a conversation well.

Just as a doctor, engineer, lawyer, or computer programmer will only achieve success by working on *himself*, similarly we can only become successful in conversation by paying constant attention to our conversational habits and by refining and improving conversational technique.

So you will come to appreciate how much more pleasant and easy contact becomes with colleagues, business associates, superiors and subordinates, and even also with friends and acquaintances, when one has learnt the proper use of language – the simplest of all means of communication.

PART ONE

Prerequisites for a discussion

CHAPTER I

The desire to speak to the other person

The skilful arranging of words and sentences does not in itself make a conversation. The most important factor in conducting a conversation is the basic attitude – towards the conversation itself and towards the other party. A person who really wants to communicate with someone else is always capable of winning him over.

1 Partner and not opponent in the conversation

You probably know the situation well: while travelling on business, you are sitting one evening on your own in a restaurant. The meal has been ordered. Suddenly the waiter appears with another guest and enquires courteously whether the gentleman might sit at your table. A short scrutinising glance. The reply – "Oh, yes certainly" – a more defensive than welcoming gesture. For a while one stares rather fixedly past the other person. After a short time the first contact occurs: smoking, the weather, the menu, the atmosphere of the restaurant and similar commonplace things. These are only preliminaries leading up to the decisive question. And the decisive question of course is: who is the other person? The conversation is consciously manoeuvred with a view to resolving this question, generally by asking what the other person is in fact doing in this place. Usually business, and on the basis of this knowledge the next question can be formulated: who, or rather what, is he?

I have never been able to avoid, for more than five minutes, answering this question.

What is the reason for this enquiry about professional occupation. Interest in the other person? An attempt to find a topic of conversation? Or perhaps merely a polite way of appearing interested? It is none of these. The question is a conscious attempt at classification. Where does he stand? Is he economically, professionally, culturally above me or below me? What consequences will this have for me in the ensuing conversation? Should I take the following line? "What you say there is very interesting. . . ." "I have never seen things in that light before. . . ." "If I might ask this question as a layman. . . .?" Or can I respond to the other person by saying: "No you have the wrong idea there. . . ." "In that case one must . . ." "Surely one should . . ." "Then you can only . . ." My position must be established, so that the course of the conversation is clear.

Perhaps you will ask: What happens when both parties are equally matched? There is no such thing as two equally matched people. If the initial approach results in an apparent match, there are continued attempts to discover the weaknesses of the other person. Perhaps he drives the smaller car, or lives in a less fashionable area, or perhaps his last summer holidays were more limited in scope than one's own. At some point or other one person is bound to expose the weakness which automatically establishes the other as superior.

I have often wondered about the motives for such behaviour. It appears to stem from our authoritarian pattern of education. Have you noticed the first words uttered by most small children? Naturally "Mama", "Dada" are the very first. And what comes next? The simple little word "no". And why the word "no"? Because it is the word which children tend to hear most frequently. Our education is essentially prohibitive. Those in authority may forbid. And authority lies with those who adopt certain attitudes towards a child. Parents, grandparents, the landlord, the policeman, to give only a few examples. The child's first impressions receive confirmation at school. There the right to issue commands and prohibitive instructions is transferred to the teacher by virtue of his official position. This right is exercised during subsequent training by the instructor or master.

One gradually becomes accustomed to living according to a system of social dependencies. But one also learns that this social system demands that one should observe certain patterns of behaviour. The expectations of society are deferred to in the "manoeuvring" outlined above. Conversations cannot be conducted on the basis of attitudes such as these. The first and most important prerequisite for each conversation is the readiness to recognise the other person as a partner, and indeed as a partner on an equal footing. No one can force me to talk to Mr. Jones. But if I do talk to Mr. Jones, then Mr. Jones is my partner. We are together, on the same level. In a conversation there is no "above" and no "below". Every conversation is a form of recognition which I accord to the other participant. Every conversation enriches me. For this I should be grateful to the other person.

A conversation should never be a contest. Conversation means co-operation. Even a disagreement must be borne along by the spirit of co-operation.

2 The desire to talk implies the ability to listen

Head of Department Smallfuss has been trying desperately for three weeks to gain access to the director. Finally he achieves his aim. The director explains volubly with dozens of superficial excuses why he has not had time in three weeks to talk to Smallfuss. Then comes the patronising question: "Well, what is on your mind?" Smallfuss begins. He has a briefcase stuffed with documents, every one of which needs to be discussed with the director. The director reclines in his armchair in relaxed fashion, folds his hands over his stomach and appears to be listening for one minute, two minutes and then his eyes gradually take on a glazed aspect, staring straight through Mr. Smallfuss. Smallfuss continues speaking for another minute. He pauses expectantly. Now the director comes to life. He straightens up: "By the way – my dear Smallfuss – in case I forget, have you taken a look at last month's telephone bill?"

At this point the conversation collapses. Of course Mr. Smallfuss knows nothing about the telephone bill. In fact there is nothing much to know about it.

It is not this lack of knowledge which causes the conversation to break down, but the realisation by Mr. Smallfuss that nothing he had said up to this point had got through to the director. As soon as Mr. Smallfuss had entered the director's office, some mechanism was activated in the latter's brain which said "Smallfuss – what about the telephone bill?" Instead of listening, the director's sole preoccupation was with the moment when he could introduce his own topic of conversation.

Since Smallfuss was not able to answer the director's question, the director is dissatisfied; and because Smallfuss was not able to gain a hearing for his problems from his superior, he too is dissatisfied. What caused this situation?

No conversation really took place here, only a monologue. One of the basic requirements for a conversation, in addition to the ability and readiness to talk, is the willingness to listen and to concern oneself with the other person. Many conversations and numerous misunderstandings in private and commercial life could be cleared up – or would never arise in the first place – if the people concerned were prepared to listen to each other and to discuss the points at issue in a reciprocal manner. Any solicitor will confirm that a great number of disputes in civil law, be they divorce proceedings, rent disputes, interpretation of contracts, or disputes over wills, have their origin in a lack of willingness to listen and to become genuinely concerned with the opposite side. We shall be returning to this subject of listening later on.

3 Even a conversation needs an ultimate aim

Ask employees of a firm, as they return from a two or three hour session in the manager's office or the conference room, what the result of these talks was. Shrugging of shoulders. "We still don't know what the manager really wanted." "Well, there was an awful lot of talking, but we didn't arrive at any result." "Nothing was finally settled, a few things still have to be looked into and we'll be discussing the matter again sometime."

Why are conversations such as these unproductive and unsatisfactory? Because we frequently embark upon talks in which the actual aim and purpose is not clear to any of the participants.

Do I wish to impart information to my partner or do I wish to obtain it from him? Do I want to advise him or am I seeking his advice? Am I trying to persuade him to make a certain decision, or have I taken a decision and now wish to communicate and explain it to him? Whatever the purpose may be, the conversation must in every case be subordinated to this purpose.

The aim of discussions should be clear to all participants. If those entering into talks have conflicting opinions as to their object, the result will either be the monologue already described or annoyance on the part of those who were unable to make their ideas prevail.

So often those engaged in discussions "lose the thread", and end up talking about completely unrelated matters. Talks must be held in a conclusive manner. This "thread" is the bond which connects the starting-point and the goal of the talks. If there is no goal in sight, then there can be no thread. The aim and purpose should not be lost sight of at any point during the talks.

To summarise, the inner attitude which is the key to every conversation is determined by the following factors:

1 The acknowledgement of the other person as a partner
2 The readiness to listen
3 The acknowledged aim of the conversation

CHAPTER II

Choose the right people to negotiate with

A suitable combination of people is an important factor in carrying out meaningful and successful negotiations. Identifying *who* to talk to has a decisive influence on their direction and outcome.

1 It is easier to talk to people who have no authority at all

This saying is attributed to the banker Herman Abs. What it means is that it is easier to have a straightforward discussion if one is not responsible for the consequences arising from it. Such discussions, however, start and finish inconclusively. A pity that so much time is spent on them!

The question of competence to carry out negotiations is one which should be applied first and foremost to oneself. Am I qualified to conduct them? In other words, does the subject of the intended discussions fall within the scope of my own duties in the company? Might subjects arise in the course of the discussions which belong more properly to the sphere of activity of my colleagues or superiors? What is the object of the discussions and do I possess the degree of competence necessary to realise this object?

If the intended talks touch upon the duties or authorities of another department within the organisation, then this department must be represented in the talks, or I must obtain permission from this department to represent them. If I, as the representative of a machine tool factory, engage in preliminary sales negotiations with a customer, then I must be clear as to what subjects can be discussed in these talks. I would have to expect a discussion of the possible uses and applications of the machine. The salesman must be in a position to put forward the arguments for his product. Should specific technical problems occur, however (for instance, in connection with other machines on the market, or particular problems relating to foundations), then I ought to realise that I do not possess the specialist knowledge necessary to discuss them. I must either obtain the assistance of a colleague from a technical department, or I must see to it that this special problem is examined by competent staff in my own company, with a view to submitting a specialist's suggestions to the customer.

Another point which can arise is the question of delivery date. The delivery date is not exclusively a matter for the sales department, since it also relates to production capacity. Thus in preparing for the talks I should ascertain ideas on delivery dates from the production or planning department. And finally, prices and conditions of payment might be a subject of these preliminary talks. Prices are either list prices or those worked out by the estimates department. I must know whether and to what extent I can deviate from these standard prices during the negotiations. The same applies to conditions of payment.

In this way I should work out the limits of my authority, so that I will be able to conduct the talks with real effectiveness without exceeding these limits.

There is often difficulty in finding a suitable person with whom to negotiate. The other participant should also have a firm idea of the extent to which certain statements may be regarded as binding and where the limits to this obligation are to be drawn.

It is therefore recommended to establish clearly, either before or immediately at the start of the talks the respective limits of authority and competence which might be of significance.

The belief that all authority resides at the top, and that one will achieve one's aim most effectively by starting discussions right at the top, is frequently misguided. The office equipment salesman who goes straight to the managing director should not be surprised if he not only insults the director by such presumptuous behaviour, but gets an unenthusiastic response from the purchasing officer who resents the attempt at under-cutting his authority. In some cases, if the salesman even has the nerve to ask the managing director to make a recommendation to the purchasing department, this could be the beginning of the end of any business relationship.

How do I reach the *right* person? Here, as in all other situations relating to talks, frankness takes precedence over tactics. The best course of action is to inform the prospective negotiator, when arranging the appointment, as to the limits of one's competence. The question: "What subjects are we competent to discuss and what will be the scope of our negotiations?" is no longer regarded as an improper question.

A fundamental mistake which is regrettably made again and again is the pretence of having authority which one does not in fact possess. Imagine this situation; you have been negotiating hard for several hours for conclusion of a contract and a formula has finally been reached regarding prices, conditions of payment and delivery, fringe considerations to which you are just able to consent. At this point your opposite number announces, radiant with satisfaction: "Thank you very much, I will now submit this draft agreement to my company, and you will be hearing from us again!" Not only this man himself, but the entire company will be suspect as far as future negotiations are concerned.

In business discussions you are not a private individual but a representative of your firm. It is your firm which is ultimately answerable for your personal errors, your playing for time, or even your deceitfulness.

Lesson: Clear demarcation of the limits of your own competence and that of the man you are negotiating with is essential.

2 Specialists among themselves

"It is true that I know much, but I should like to know everything," Goethe has Wagner say in Faust. The pipe-dream of universal knowledge has long faded. Today individual areas of knowledge are so extensive and differentiated that it is no longer possible even to gain an overall view of each area. Indeed, complete mastery of a single area of knowledge is in itself a considerable challenge. This fact should always be borne in mind on entering into negotiations. It is still commonplace to find company employees, particularly in the upper echelons of management, who have difficulty in admitting their ignorance on a certain point. A favourite tactic is to reel off a string of generalisations, in lieu of the specialist knowledge which they do not in fact possess.

This only serves to weaken a position in negotiation. The other participant, possibly himself a highly trained specialist, can easily ascertain the degree of specialist knowledge which his opponent possesses by occasionally interjecting a pointed question in the course of the conversation. If he should discover the weaknesses or, shall we say, vanity of the other, the discussion will sooner or later take an unpleasant turn for the charlatan.

It is part of the preparatory phase of negotiations to consider whether and at what stage in the talks specialised questions might arise which the person responsible may be inadequately equipped to handle. It should also be decided whether, in view of the anticipated technical questions, an informative briefing should take place before the main talks, with the man conducting the negotiations himself answering the questions, or whether it is more suitable to enlist the aid of the relevant specialist.

I would recommend the latter alternative. Specialists have their own language. They can reach an understanding among themselves better and more quickly if involved initially, rather than being consulted at a later stage. To bring them in later can result in considerable misunderstanding and confusion, and in certain circumstances can also have very costly consequences.

I can recall the concluding of a large foreign contract which was being negotiated at board level. The board member concerned, who was not in the foreign trade section, asked the head of the foreign department to draw up a summary sheet containing a large number of questions which would have to be clarified in connection with this particular transaction. In addition, the head of the foreign department gave the board member a short talk on the subject. The board member took notes. However, the head of the foreign department did not mention currency, and the necessity arose in the board negotiations of using a third currency as a basis for calculation. For this the other side had fixed the exchange rate of their own currency in relation to this third currency, while the director of my own organisation omitted to do so. In so doing, he had taken upon himself the entire risk relating to the exchange rate. It was only possible to limit this risk to some extent by means of subsequent and expensive dealings designed to guarantee the exchange rate security. The director had appreciated all the commercial risks involved and had taken them into consideration when drawing up the contract, but he was unfamiliar with the problems and risks relating to currency, so he overlooked a vital point.

If specialised questions arise during talks, whether they be technical, financial or legal questions, it is necessary to decide what significance they will have for the outcome of the negotiations. If they are highly specialised and of subordinate importance in relation to the general technical content of the talks, they should be abstracted and left to the relevant specialists for analysis. However, if they are relevant to other subjects under discussion, it is better to discontinue the talks and resume them after clarification of the technicalities, rather than to continue the talks on a hypothetical basis. A hypothetical discussion is an interesting intellectual exercise, but yields no concrete results and merely delays and complicates further negotiations.

Always leave specialised problems to the specialists.

3 How does one negotiate at managing director level?

The sense and nonsense involved in the hierarchical structure of a company is a subject open to debate. You may like it or you may not. Whatever one may think, this form of company structure is still with us and as long as it exists, it has certain consequences, not only within the particular organisation, but also on a company to company basis. While it is possible in one's own company to blur the distinction between hierarchical levels by means of good management, these gradations often play an important role in the relationship of one company to another. After all, both managing directors and middle managers find it easier to reach an understanding with people of their own rank than for instance the managing director of company A with a middle manager of company B. Thus, the social status of the persons involved can influence the success or failure of negotiations.

Take the following case. As a branch manager of a bank in a small town you refer the self-confident owner of a large (by local standards) company with a share capital of £100, to a clerk saying that the clerk is competent to deal with such matters. You incur the displeasure not only of this company owner but through him of other people of account in the town. His bank negotiations elevate or downgrade him socially according to whether he conducts them with the branch manager himself or only with a senior clerk.

The decision about who to negotiate with, as discussed previously, is in practice limited if one of the people concerned insists on talking to someone of equal status. Then it is the task of the person who is equal in social rank but is not competent on specialised subjects, to build up a competent but socially inferior employee in his own company in such a way that in future he will be accepted as a suitable man to negotiate with.

How can this be achieved? There are two possibilities. I, as managing director, can conduct the discussion in very general terms. When it begins to get down to specifics, I can suggest that the details should be discussed between an employee which my opposite number may wish to delegate for this purpose and "my specialist in the subject, Mr. X". The second possibility is that I have my competent member of staff present at the talks from the very beginning and attempt to draw him into the conversation whenever specialised subjects arise. Such phrases as: "I am not really very well versed in this subject, I think we had better ask Mr. Cooper who is our specialist", used sufficiently often – but not too obviously – convey the impression that in future it would be much more productive to confer with my Mr. Cooper rather than with me.

If, however, there is too great a discrepancy in social status between the two persons involved the conversation will be embarrassing for the socially inferior person. In such a case I would want the talks held between two persons of equal status, even if they are without specialist competence.

What is actually meant by equal social status? From the turnover and profit points of view, the head of department in a large store may surpass the largest private retailer of the same trade in his area, but nevertheless remains a head of department, while the other is a proprietor of his own business. One should not, however, concern oneself with form or class but rather with similarity of function.

4 Top level negotiations

Many people believe that talks carried on at top level are easier, not only because of the content of the talks, but also because such talks can result in a clear conclusion. But it is at this very level that decision-making becomes particularly complicated. Parkinson and Peter have drawn attention to this and have attributed it to a lack of inclination to make decisions. Frequently, however, it is not a question of lack of inclination to make decisions or of readiness to discuss a transaction with finality, but rather the greater number of legal restrictions. These often make conclusive talks at this level fundamentally more difficult than they would be on lower levels. One would therefore do well not to believe blindly that all competence resides at the top level.

Summarising, it can be stated: The correct man to negotiate with is the person who is completely competent, possesses suitable specialist knowledge, is adequate in rank and can conduct talks in a professional manner which will result in a definite conclusion.

CHAPTER III

Mental and physical prerequisites for negotiations

For many forms of employment it is taken for granted that a person must in the first instance possess certain physical or mental capabilities. The polisher in a metal works, the furniture remover, the fisherman on board a trawler, all must have certain physical capabilities in order to meet the demands placed on them by their employment. They need strength and endurance. Likewise a suitable mental disposition is obviously a necessary prerequisite for the occupation of nurse, truck driver or judge. The required attributes are sympathy, tolerance and the ability to establish contact. However, everyone is expected to be able to carry on a conversation in whatever circumstances. "Williams, go to the general manager's office, please," is the brief request. No one enquires whether Williams is in good health, or whether he has just dragged himself to the office suffering from flu. The general manager does not ask whether Williams is perhaps weighed down by worries due to the death of a close relative or differences of opinion with a colleague. Williams must now take part in discussions, and at the best receive a reproof for having so little concentration today. To overlook the prerequisites for a good discussion can only result in a negative outcome.

What conditions must be fulfilled in order that the participants in a discussion can feel completely relaxed and equal to the situation?

1 Impartiality towards oneself

Anyone wishing to conduct a good discussion must feel free and confident, free and impartial with regard to his own attitudes and confident in the subject which he is to discuss.

(a) Do I feel qualified for this particular discussion?

Whenever I enter into negotiations I should ask myself the question: Do I feel qualified for these talks? And this implies a further question: What demands will be placed on me? For instance, what subjects could be discussed? How broad is the range which could be treated? Am I well enough informed to deal with all questions? Have I enough specialised knowledge to put forward my case effectively and do I feel confident to apply my knowledge convincingly?

A feeling of being inadequately qualified results in a tense attitude which in turn manifests itself as aggressiveness. On the other hand, confidence shows itself in relaxation and command of the situation. Unfortunately, again and again one finds in business that younger colleagues put themselves in situations for which they possess neither the specialist competence nor negotiating skill. Consequently they allow themselves to be provoked, which is inevitably to the disadvantage of their organisation.

(b) Am I convinced about what I intend to say?

I can only have a free and independent attitude with regard to my opposite number if I identify myself completely with the viewpoint I wish to express. Take the following example. You return home in the evening completely worn out. You are greeted at the front door by your wife who admonishes: "You must tell Tommy that he must stop playing football with his friends every afternoon because I just can't go on washing his things every evening." At this point your own tender years come to mind and all the scoldings you were treated to on those occasions. You understand little Tommy only too well, and you also understand only too well what he feels about his mother's scolding. None the less, you are obliged to maintain parental authority and have a talk with him. After your first two or three sentences the brat has already realised what your attitude to the subject really is. He interjects a couple of questions and you go into a skid. The carefully feigned speech bursts like a soap bubble.

If a person lacks conviction about what he intends to say, it is better that he says nothing at all. This principle is defensible when applied to one's own private affairs. But the matter becomes rather more complex when one is unable to identify with the views which must be put forward as representative of a company. I am thinking particularly of the salesman who has to sell a piece of equipment which he knows to have certain disadvantages when applied as its purchaser intends; also of the branch manager of a credit company who, contrary to the recommendations he has made to head office, must now inform a good client that his application for an increase in credit has been refused; and of the refusal to accept a complaint from a customer although one is convinced that it is justified.

These and hundreds of other situations result in a conflict of conscience which is a considerable burden for the person who has to express the prescribed attitude. In this case, he must either have the moral courage to declare quite openly what he feels himself or, if he cannot do that, he must stifle his reservations and represent the interests of his company as forcibly as possible.

(c) Have I more important things on my mind?

Negotiations demand the complete concentration of the participants. This means that at the specific time and place when they occur there is not and should not be anything more important for the participants than the negotiations themselves. A person preoccupied with personal or business worries cannot conduct good negotiations. A person who has been torn away from a job of work requiring complete concentration in order to conduct negotiations which he regards as less important will have at most only a half-hearted interest in the talks. The results will inevitably be less satisfactory for the company concerned.

The freedom mentioned above relates not only to the subject but also to the personality of the participants in talks. I must be prepared to establish contact. In the personal sphere I can choose who I talk to and who are my friends. This is not always possible in business. I must accept the person who is presented to me for commercial reasons. Sympathy and antipathy towards him must be subordinated to the aim of the talks. Should I feel unable to negotiate with a particular person, I should quite openly inform my superior of this fact. Under no circumstances should the business at hand be allowed to suffer because of personal antipathy.

(*d*) *Am I physically fit enough to undertake these talks?*

This is an obvious point. Nevertheless, it should be mentioned once again. I can only enter into talks when I feel in complete possession of my mental and physical powers. Yes indeed, there *are* physical requirements which must be fulfilled. How often have I arrived at the appointed time for talks with a customer only to be greeted with the words: "Don't come too near, I have terrible 'flu, a temperature of 101° this morning. If we hadn't already arranged these talks I would have stayed at home and gone to bed." If only he had stayed in bed! The talks which ensue are most unlikely to produce concrete results.

A conversation which is constantly interrupted by coughing and sneezing, accompanied by profuse apologies and references to his unfortunate state of health, is not a pleasure either for the healthy or the sick person. In most cases it is quite fruitless, is discontinued after a relatively short time and must be resumed at a later date. One must be in good health when undertaking negotiations. Talks are a form of work. Reference has already been made to this fact. Work is generally associated with exertion and exertion causes fatigue. Therefore every discussion is accompanied by signs of fatigue. These indicate diminished levels of concentration.

When I embark upon negotiations I must know the length of time for which I can sustain concentration. It is necessary to study one's own powers of concentration, since these may vary in different situations. The ability to concentrate depends on the subject under discussion, on the persons involved in the conversation and last but not least on the actual time at which the conversation takes place. Anyone who has to engage in many rounds of talks must focus his complete attention on these activities and as far as possible must adapt his conversational style to the circumstances.

Time and again one encounters businessmen who start negotiations with a real display of fireworks. They exercise a captivating charm. They positively scintillate with ideas. Their arguments are so convincing that it seems impossible to withhold approval. But after a short time the fireworks have burnt out. The brilliant debater of the first ten minutes becomes a tedious, carping know-all which he remains for the rest of the discussion. This deline in performance not only disillusions the other participants, but it also exposes the particular weaknesses of the dazzler. It is important to be able to maintain one's conversational style for the duration of the talks.

2 Independent objectivity towards other people

Just as I must feel free and objective with regard to myself during negotiations, I also need a minimum degree of freedom with regard to whoever I am negotiating with. This means nothing more than feeling independent of the course of the conversation.

(a) What room for manoeuvre do I have at my disposal?

Every discussion moves between two extremes. There is the question of what do I wish to avoid at all costs? And there is the question what do I wish to talk about? The conversation must be carried on between these two poles, and in such a way that it achieves the greatest possible distance from the negative point of departure and is directed as close as possible to the desired positive resolution.

To take an example, my clerk Williams has applied for the post of head of section which has become vacant. I may consider Williams to be a first-class senior clerk but think that he lacks the necessary qualifications to become a section head. In other words: I would like to keep him as a senior clerk and do not wish to promote him to head of section. What are the extreme positions in this situation? The most extreme negative reaction would be for Williams to resign due to my rejection of him as a candidate for the post of section head. The most positive reaction would be for Williams to declare his satisfaction with this decision.

Establishing room for manoeuvre in a conversation is an essential part of preparation beforehand. When I enter into this conversation, therefore, I have consciously accepted the possibility that Williams might resign. I should not be at all afraid of this consequence. The technique of negotiation is concerned with discouraging Williams as far as possible from this negative reaction and encouraging him to react positively. With this end in view, I decide what subjects I will not discuss with Williams and which subjects I will discuss of my own accord. For instance, I will not discuss the possibility of resignation or the possible consequences which such a resignation would have. My talk must be structured in such a way that this matter is not mentioned at all.

On the other hand, there are many constructive things I can say with reference to what measures must be taken in future so that Williams will one day be able to assume leadership of a section. When I appreciate the range within which I can manoeuvre it is much easier for me to construct the conversation within these admissible limits. If, on the other hand, I had been instructed to inform Williams that he cannot become a section head in our company, but at all costs prevent his resignation, then the latitude in the talks would be practically nil.

(b) Am I in agreement with the limitations imposed by my instructions?

A friend of mine in the credit business recently told me about the following case. A young and promising employee has been asking him, the head of the branch, for quite some time to allow him to handle a large deal on his own responsibility. One day a fixed deposit of £125,000 became payable. The branch manager thought this would be a suitable opportunity for his junior. He therefore requested the young employee to have talks with the commercial manager of an important local company regarding extension of the fixed deposit. Since in the meantime there had been a drop in the fixed deposit interest rate, he instructed the employee not to go below $8\frac{1}{2}$ per cent but at all costs to make sure that the client was not driven away.

The talks between the employee and the company owner took place as scheduled. The branch manager looked at his watch. More than an hour passed and the talks still continued. The branch manager considered that talks of this nature should not last more than ten minutes. Thereupon he entered his employee's office and found the customer and his employee in a violent dispute about the rate of interest. The client was not satisfied with 8½ per cent. The clerk could not and would not grant more than the prescribed 8¼ per cent. The branch manager explained to me: "I then entered into the conversation, and the whole thing was settled in two minutes. The client left the £750,000 with us on the basis of 8½ per cent. Now I ask you, what is the point of leaving such talks to one's employees?"

I asked: ' Well, what did you say to the client?" He replied: "I told the client quite definitely, that I would not give him more than 8¼ per cent. If he was not prepared to do business on this basis then we would have to forget about the whole transaction." Then I asked: "And what would have happened if the client had withdrawn his business?" To which the branch manager replied: "Then I wouldn't have been able to do anything about it." I asked: "And what would you have done if your employee had come to you and said that the client had not accepted the 8¼ per cent, and that he had withdrawn the money?" The manager's answer: "Well, I would certainly have had something to say about that!" Then I said to him: "You see, and because your employee knew that, his talks lasted more than an hour, and you were able to settle things in two minutes".

This small example demonstrates that in a discussion with a predetermined objective, the person representing the objective must consider it possible to realise this aim. When this objective is inseparably linked to the necessity for success, the result will either be indifference or stress.

If an employee is given unrealistic sales targets to achieve he will conduct his sales talks thinking: "I will never achieve the target anyway, so it doesn't really matter if I remain 5 or 10 per cent below the required level – I will get into hot water in any case." It is therefore important that the declared objectives of talks held on behalf of the company appear to be attainable by the employee in question, and that he should identify himself with this objective. He can enter into talks with a certain attitude of authority if he has achieved this identification.

(c) Am I afraid of the other party?

I have already mentioned this question: in private life we can select those we hold discussions with according to our mutual sympathies, antipathies and other attitudes. This is not possible in the business sphere. We have no choice about those we have to negotiate with. There are certain people with whom we can "get on". One person prefers to negotiate with a quiet and logical type of person and is afraid of people who become excited and hammer on the desk with their fists. Another prefers the cynical type; others fear the quiet tactician. How does one come to terms with such emotional reactions?

Why is a child afraid of thunder? Because it does not know the physical processes which cause lightning and thunder, and because it cannot yet see how to protect itself from such natural phenomena. This judgement can also be applied to negotiators. Fear implies ignorance of the motives on which the actions and attitudes of the other are based. It also implies a lack of insight into the various means of protecting oneself from certain attitudes.

Conversation is to a great extent an exercise in practical psychology. Anyone who wishes to conduct successful discussions has to concern himself with the causes of certain patterns of behaviour. An essential factor in establishing one's objective independence in relation to others is to recognise the type of attitude favoured by the other party and to adapt one's own attitude accordingly.

CHAPTER IV

Mode and style of speaking

The essence of conversation is the spoken word. These words do not usually issue from the mouth of the speaker in a haphazard manner, but are consciously formed and controlled. Speech is the conscious forming of words and the controlled arrangement of words into sentences, the consecutive organisation of related sentences and finally the communication of one's own thoughts to someone else by virtue of these interrelated sentences.

1 Breathing is something to learn

Breathing is a subconscious process. It is only when difficulties arise, for instance diseases of the respiratory organs or shortness of breath, that one becomes fully conscious of the fact that one is continually breathing. However, it is possible to exercise conscious control over one's breathing processes. One can hold breath when diving, breathe more slowly or quickly at will, and perform certain exercises in concentration by means of breath control.

The fact that one can control respiration in a conscious manner should be put to use in conversation. The important thing is to use breathing to achieve increased effectiveness of speech. To put breathing to full effect, it is necessary to know what reserves of air are at one's disposal. There is a series of exercises by means of which this can be checked. The simplest way is to select any text and read it without interruption for as long as the reserves of air allow, without having to force the voice and without experiencing difficulty in breathing in again. When one has thus established the reserves of air available, one can proceed to a second experiment.

Are these reserves of air sufficient to make the association of ideas within a sentence or the continuity of concept in a thought which one wishes to express more effective by means of breath control? Inadequate reserves of air and uncontrolled breathing result in a disjointed flow of speech, which not only disfigures the clearest and most attractive thoughts, but after a time has an acoustically disturbing effect on the person listening and makes it difficult for him to follow the train of thought.

The reserves of air at one's disposal are not a fact that one must simply accept. Breath volume can be increased by performing suitable exercises.

The state of one's breathing also has a psychological effect. Breathing out relaxes, breathing in causes tension. The old saying: "Take a deep breath and into the boss" is nonsense. If one follows this piece of advice, one enters the discussion in a state of tension, physically and psychologically. Quite the contrary, one should approach the opposing party in a state of exhalation. Exhalation relaxes the muscles and also induces psychological relaxation, therefore increasing receptivity.

Breathing has another aspect. Normally two people conversing are far enough apart so that the breath of one does not reach the other. But this is not always the case. For instance, two people bending over a drawing or plan together, or studying a table of figures, are in very close proximity. It is important that one is not repelled by the breath of the other. Care should therefore be taken about bad breath. This can have many causes and only a doctor can help in such cases.

There are, however, forms of breath odour over which one can exercise personal control. The principal causes here are alcohol and nicotine. Before meeting for talks one should not take any forms of alcohol which result in strong breath odour. If it is impossible to avoid imbibing alcohol its smell should be disguised by such remedies as peppermint or mouth spray. The same situation arises with intensive use of nicotine. Continuous cigar smoking has a bad effect on the breath. The advice given above applies in this case. A person rarely notices his own bad breath. It is therefore better to take some preventive measure than to wait until one is discreetly informed by a third party – a client or secretary for instance.

2 . . . The rain in Spain falls mainly on the plain . . . (Pronunciation)

Do you remember "My Fair Lady" and the despairing attempts of Professor Higgins to give Eliza Doolittle a good English accent? It is also said: "Manners maketh man; not birth." Speech is a means of communication and communication to a large extent means comprehension. This comprehension has a double meaning. In the first place the listener must be able to take in the words of the speaker in an acoustic sense; and secondly his comprehension of the words should enable him to understand the idea or the thought behind those words.

I must therefore ask myself how I ought to speak in order to make myself understood by the other person.

Pronunciation should be clear. Words should be enunciated distinctly. It is a bad habit to slur over the ends of one's words or to distort words to the point of senselessness by mutilating them or running them together. In practice one does not say: "Let us go out"; one says: "Lessgo out"! "That is a", in ordinary colloquial speech sounds like: "Thatsa". Such disfigurations of speech make an uncultivated impression and are repellent to the ear. Although speech should be clear, this does not mean that it should be affected. A conversation is not a stage performance.

It is unfortunate that when we are speaking we are unaware of how we are speaking and whether we are articulating our words clearly and comprehensibly for those listening. It is essential for those who have to conduct many conversations to check on the quality of their speech from time to time by means of tape recordings or, even better, video-recordings.

3 I prefer a cultivated baritone (Pitch of voice)

Volume is an important factor in understanding speech. The average volume of speech employed in a conversation must be such that the listener is able to follow what is being spoken without undue exertion or repeated questioning. Excessively loud speech gives an impression of aggressiveness, excitation and not infrequently insecurity. Quiet speech gives the impression of tiredness, and is difficult for the listener to follow. Repeated questioning becomes necessary, which interrupts the flow of the conversation and after a while results in indifference.

Maintaining a normal level of volume does not however mean that a conversation has to drone on in complete phonetic regularity. It is this very normality of volume which allows the speaker to modulate his speech. It is possible to increase suspense and attentiveness by reducing volume and slowing down one's speech. Certain ideas can be emphasised by applying acoustic stress at the appropriate point. One can provide a background to one's train of thought by increasing and reducing volume where desired, similar to the crescendo and diminuendo in music.

Besides volume, the rate of speech must also be controlled in conversation. The chosen speed must be attuned to the fact that the listener has to assimilate something new, perhaps completely unknown, and he must process it mentally. Most people talk too quickly, particularly when they have prepared themselves well. Speaking quickly gives the listener an impression of nervousness, insecurity, and even that the speaker has learnt his words by heart. On the other hand excessively slow speech gives a fatigued impression and impedes concentration. A normal rate of speaking allows us to pronounce individual words clearly and comprehensibly. The normal tempo of speech should make it possible for the speaker to change speed if desired. A change in rhythm can decisively increase the effectiveness of speech.

Finally, a word about the pitch of one's voice. High voices sound shrill and aggressive. They place excessive acoustic demands on the listener. On the other hand, deep voices have a soothing effect and inspire confidence, but are rarely soporific or boring. The most favourable pitch of voice for conversation is the baritone. It is pleasant to listen to, it is economical in breath requirements and it also allows modulations in an upward or downward direction to give acoustic emphasis to the spoken words.

A very important factor in speaking – one which is frequently underestimated – is the pause. It is a means by which the speaker can arrange his conversation. Related ideas are expressed together. The termination of a train of thought is underlined by means of a brief pause. Also a pause in conversation allows the listener to assimilate the thoughts expressed, to think them over, to remove misunderstandings by relevant questions or to enter into a discussion.

The pause helps the speaker to concentrate his attention on the next idea to be expressed and to formulate it in advance. An uninterrupted flow of speech has an unnatural effect, rather like a recitation. Speech without pause sometimes gives the impression that the listener is not supposed to think about what is being said at all. He is simply to be talked into the ground. He is to be robbed of any opportunity of examining the other person's proposition by asking specific questions or raising objections. This is the conversational style of the bad salesman, the town crier or the political agitator.

4 Not everything one says is fit for print

Several years ago I happened to hear a friend of mine making a speech on a subject which was very topical at the time. I, like most of those listening, was so impressed that I said I would be prepared to revise the speech for printing. This was made simpler by the fact that the whole address was recorded on tape. However, when I received a transcript a few days later I was appalled. What I found written down was a disjointed mass of words. Then I listened to the recording of the speech once more and was impressed just as favourably as at the first hearing. I edited the transcript into standard English. Then I asked a friend who expressed complete agreement with my written version to record it on tape. The result was shattering. The impetus and urgency which distinguished the original speech were lost.

It cannot be over-emphasised that the spoken word and the written word are completely different in their effect. The listener thinks in a different way from the reader. The listener wishes to be engulfed by words. He wishes to allow a thought to take hold of him in its totality. He is under the sway of the personality of the person speaking with all his gestures, intonation, modulation, pitch of voice, etc. In short, with the listener, appeal is made not only to the reason, but also to the entire range of emotions.

By contrast the reader is alone with his text; the author is remote behind his written words. Combinations of words and thoughts are analysed more critically. The emotions come in only peripherally.

It would seem that few people are conscious of this fundamental distinction. The judgement that what he says is "almost ready for the press" is still regarded as a compliment. Have you ever listened to anyone whose speeches are almost good enough for printing? It is a tiring experience.

I should like to state once again: there are no formulas for achieving a good style of speech. Both speech and style of expression are part and parcel of the personality of the person who is speaking. The style of speech must be in tune with his personality. He must be able to interpret it with complete credibility. Do not attempt to copy the speech of a well-known politician, a famous actor or a popular television newsreader. You will not obtain their effect. Everyone who conducts frequent negotiations must develop his own individual style. However, there are certain guide-lines for evolving one's own style, and these are discussed below.

Speech should be cultivated. What is "cultivation" in language? You cultivate your appearance. How do you do that? You take care that your clothes are clean, you see that there is no dirt or stain on your jacket. You make sure that no buttons are missing and that no edges have frayed, that your handkerchief is clean and your shoes polished. You pay this kind of attention to your everyday clothing and even your casual wear. The important thing for you is that no one should be offended by small signs of sartorial neglect.

Now transfer this idea to speech. Your speech can also show signs of neglect, specks of dirt, missing buttons, frayed edges. This applies to your everyday speech, the language you use in business, and also your language on the sports field.

What are the weak points in language which require special attention? The choice of words and ideas. Stay in your own world with the words and concepts you already use. Don't go borrowing and making excursions to areas which you do not understand. If I wish to convince my customer of the advantages of a new detergent, it is not necessary for me to enter the conceptual sphere of computer technology or nuclear physics.

Almost every profession has developed its own language. Every organisation and within the larger organisations every department develops its own language. This is only spoken within the milieu. Words which set off ideas and associations in this milieu are met with incomprehension, even rejection, in other surroundings.

Without doubt it is an intellectual achievement if one of the participants in a discussion succeeds in constructing and bringing to a correct grammatical conclusion a sentence lasting for two minutes. For the listener upon whom it is inflicted, however, it is an imposition.

Kurt Tucholsky begins his advice for good orators with the appeal: main clauses, main clauses, main clauses! It is tiring to have to repeat constantly: Language must not only be spoken, it must also be understood and processed by the listener. Short sentences are easy to follow. The listener tends to lose the continuity in long compound sentences. If he loses the sense of what is being said, his interest declines. If interest declines, even the most inspiring train of thought will simply pass over him. The forming of short, clear sentences necessitates a mental discipline on the part of the speaker. Long, poorly arranged and complicated sentences are usually a sign of awkward and complicated thought processes.

Happily, speech does not yet have punctuation marks. If I wish to make a statement, ask a question, or emphasise something, I have no technical means at my disposal. It is necessary for me to replace all punctuation marks by the way in which I employ the language.

Most people have a love–hate relationship with officialdom. On the one hand the word "official" is used to express an extreme degree of narrow-mindedness, pedantry, obsequiousness, lack of

B*

readiness to assume responsibility, etc. On the other hand people copy the behaviour of the official, particularly in oral and written statements. People no longer talk of correspondence with a client but rather of "written communication". Whenever the opportunity presents itself to clip two pieces of paper together, a "procedure" is observed. Letters are no longer signed but rather a "signature is appended".

Have you ever had a *talk* with a colleague in your company? Of course not. You have "been in consultation", or you have "conferred" with him, and all the other impressive phrases originating from officialdom. Such expressions should now be obsolete.

Language must be flexible. It must contain illustrations. The listener must be able to form his own concept of the situation described. If someone says to me: "I've been talking to Miss Smith", I should be able to form a concept of this situation. I myself often talk to Miss Smith. If the same colleague comes to me and says: "I have just been in consultation with Miss Smith on such and such a matter", then I have to swallow hard. Bombastic speech is of course intended to impress. Language has a tendency towards gigantism. Listen closely to people who are generally regarded as skilful talkers. They assemble a series of words and connect these words with auxiliary verbs and a few meaningless expletives. Never say: "The table is round." This would actually mean something to the listener. Rather say: "Considering this table in its entirety, I have the inescapable impression that the form of the table seems to be that of a uniform roundness." Using such an expression, one would be sure of being elected to any club committee.

5 "Let's start at square one and say . . ." (For the sake of argument)

Have you ever attended a scientific debate? Have you ever taken part in a discussion between so-called intellectuals? If so you will already have encountered that favourite occupation: definitions. "Before we debate the subject under discussion, let us first define what we all understand by the term 'discussion' ". A discussion which starts in this way is usually concluded after three hours with a resolution to set up a committee to define once and for all the concept of discussion for future debates. A pity that so much mental energy has been squandered. Everyone involved knows quite well what is meant by discussion. Don't burden your talks with unnecessary definitions.

Naturally in every discussion everyone concerned should be quite clear as to what is being discussed. Detailed definitions should only claim attention during the course of the debate if it proves absolutely necessary. Definitions of a broad nature with a claim to general validity only serve to restrict one's scope. The desire for definition encourages dogmatism. And dogmatism is the arch-enemy of all debate.

Discussions are directed towards achieving something. For this reason, they must be conducted pragmatically. Anything which helps the discussion to reach its goal, should be included. The need for definitions must be decided in relation to the aim of the discussion.

6 Judgement or appraisal?

Some years ago a colleague reproached a subordinate with the words: "I'll decide what's logical in this firm, not you!" When I asked my angered colleague what had happened, he showed me a table which the other man had drawn up, and said: "When I asked him how he obtained that result he told me that it was completely logical."

There are many forms of logic. The specific form of logic used in a discussion is debate. The participants in a discussion reach their goal by means of logical argument. The technique of debate is therefore adapted to the goal of the discussion. Here we come back to the point mentioned earlier: a discussion needs a definite goal. A debate can only have any degree of finality if it has a declared objective.

Now a word about the structure of a discussion. There are two main styles: the "judgement" style or the "appraisal" style. The judgement style means that I make the statement which is the subject of the talk at the outset, then proceed to enumerate specific reasons. It is called judgement style because one is thereby following the traditional pattern in which a court sentence is passed. The legal formula runs: "The accused is hereby sentenced to a total period of imprisonment of . . . on the following grounds. . . ." The judgement style is usually preferred for the announcement and justification of decisions, or for particularly intensive consultations. "Mr Black, I have examined your application for an increase in salary, and must inform you that we have not agreed to it. In the course of the last few months you have . . ." Or: "I urgently recommend you to use Supershine car polish. Applying this polish gives you the additional advantage of being able to remove any bodywork damage caused during the winter."

The expert appraisal style operates in reverse order. The reasons and justifications for the decision are presented first in very general terms. The reasons are then made more specific and are eventually condensed into a definitive statement. The two above-mentioned examples, treated in the "appraisal" style, would assume the following pattern: "Mr. Black, you have been with our company for sixteen years, yet in the course of these years . . . On the basis of these deliberations I have come to the conclusion, that in your case there would be no justification for an increase in salary." And: "Last winter was particularly harsh, salt on all the roads . . . and for this purpose I would recommend to you our car-polish Supershine."

Both these types of construction have advantages and disadvantages. Imagine a court proceeding. The judge enters the courtroom and consults the jury. Solemn silence reigns. The judge declares: "The accused is sentenced to a total period of three and a half years imprisonment on the following grounds. . ." The justification of the sentence is then set forth. However, if you ask the accused immediately after the judgement has been passed the reasons why he has been sentenced, he will be unable to give you an answer. He "switched off" after the judgement was pronounced. All he was able to think about was the severity of the punishment and the possible consequences. The detailed reasons for the sentence made no impression on him.

The danger of speaking in this way in other situations is considerable. Picture the banker explaining to a customer that his application for credit has been rejected or the civil engineer saying he has decided to withdraw from a contract. In almost all situations like this the other party reacts in the same way as the accused in court and switches off.

The appraisal style also has its weak points. It often gives an impression of dishonesty. The listener may feel that the other man is looking for suitable excuses before announcing his decision. Outbursts such as: "Come on, what are you really getting at?" are unavoidable.

There is no way of guaranteeing which one of these techniques will be more effective. The effectiveness depends on the speaker and the subject of the discussion. The advantage of the "judgement" style is without doubt that the attitude adopted in the conversation is established at the outset. However, it does mean that the conversation must be very carefully prepared in advance.

I must be clear about the possible reactions of whoever I am talking to and must consider how to avoid provoking undesirable reactions. There must be scope for progress. If I announce and then proceed to justify a negative decision, the justification must be constructive. The other party must be immediately stimulated into action and drawn into the conversation. A banker receiving his client's application for an increase in credit should not explain his refusal in terms of the client's insufficient solvency or inadequate capital assets. He should rather encourage his client to discuss with him how to create the necessary preconditions for an increase in credit facilities, or what possibilities exist for achieving his business aims without increased financial assistance.

The person communicating a decision should place himself mentally in the position of the person to whom he is announcing it. The "judgement" style has a certain finality about it, and for this reason imparts an element of stiffness to the entire conversation. The "appraisal" style is more elastic. It enables one to work out general ideas with the other person step by step and allow him to draw the logical conclusions for himself.

Many years ago I witnessed a masterful display of conversational manoeuvring based on the appraisal technique. The point at issue was that I wished to build a thatched house in an area where such houses were a rarity. Special permission was necessary for this purpose, and it was well known that the housing department concerned granted few such licences. I drew up an application in my best official language which I showed to my architect. He read the application and shook his head, saying: "I think we'll do this rather differently and pay a visit to the planning department."

There he eloquently described the rustic charm of the area in which I wished to build my house. He depicted the attractiveness of the area in such glowing terms that after a short while the official in charge said of his own accord: "Well, if one wanted to build in an area like this one would really have to build a thatched house." The architect continued the conversation in this manner, so effectively that finally the official himself sat down and sketched the kind of house he imagined would be suitable for the area in question. It is almost superfluous to mention that, but for a few unimportant details, this sketch corresponded very closely to my architect's design.

The appraisal style makes it easier to bridge critical situations arising during a conversation, since it allows one to refer back repeatedly to ideas arrived at mutually during an earlier stage in the conversation, which can be used as a basis for redeveloping the conversation.

The terms "inductive" and "deductive" are often used with reference to techniques of argument. What do they mean?

A deductive argument starts with generalities, proceeds towards specific examples, and culminates in a particular conclusion.

An inductive argument operates in reverse fashion, starting with the particular expanding outwards and culminating in general conclusions.

To explain the meaning of a share, using the inductive method, one would proceed in this way: "Look, here I have a piece of paper. At the top of this piece of paper is written the name of a firm, here the word 'share' is printed, an amount of money is stated and to the right and left you can see a number of signatures. This piece of paper and the information given on it is meant to express the following . . . and a piece of paper like this is called a security."

On the other hand, if I wish to explain the meaning of a share by the deductive method, I should do it something like this: "First of all a share is a security; securities are documents which . . . etc. Thus the piece of paper before you fulfils all the necessary requirements for a share. This piece of paper is a share."

Considered from the viewpoint of conversational technique, there is no essential difference between the deductive method and the appraisal style on the one hand, and the inductive method and the judgement style on the other hand. The important thing is that the argument should be self-contained, comprehensible to the listener and directed towards the goal of the conversation. The logic of a series of statements should not have to be communicated to the listener by means of verbal explanations, but should be implicit in the structure of the argument employed.

Are my arguments reaching the listener? Don't assume that each of your arguments should follow upon one another in uninterrupted succession. Reassure yourself repeatedly during the conversation that the listener is still on the same plane as you and that no breakdown in communication has occurred. But don't ask: "Have you followed me this far?" Or: "Have I made myself understood?" Or: "I do not know whether as a specialist I have made myself sufficiently clear for a layman." Questions presented in this form detract from the status of the other person. They alienate him and not infrequently cause him to react with obstinacy.

The simplest technical aid to test the listener's comprehension is the pause. As soon as a thought or assertion is made, pause briefly. The listener should then recognise that he is being given an opportunity to ask questions or to express a differing opinion.

Another possibility is to summarise a complicated and difficult series of ideas and to repeat the main points of the argument in different terms. Avoid meaningless rhetorical questions such as "May I just summarise briefly once again?" Of course you may!

Why "again"? You have not summarised at all yet – and it will soon become clear whether the summary is brief or not. Say simply, "To summarise . . ."

The next step is the test of comprehension. One should withdraw the other person from the passive role of listener and engage him actively in conversation. Questions to test comprehension should also encourage the listener to transfer what has been said into the context of his own experience. "Have you any previous experience in this field?" "Do you think that my suggestion could be put into practice in your organisation?" "I have only touched on a few problems; do you think that there are any further aspects which should be discussed?"

Be careful. Don't be tempted into asking conjectural questions such as: "May I assume that this point has been made sufficiently clear?" It will be embarrassing if you get the reply: "None of what you have said is at all clear." Caution is also recommended when making provocative statements. Not everyone can recognise the real intention behind such statements. An assertion such as "If I know your firm, it will only start using this new technique when all the other companies are starting to scrap it" can be interpreted by the listener, according to his temperament, as an invitation to contradict the speaker or even as a piece of sheer impudence. One can only afford to utter statements like this within a close circle of friends. In business talks they are not to be recommended.

A far more likely situation than that of having to encourage the listener to speak is preventing him from constantly interrupting the conversation or relating it directly to himself by irrelevant and untimely questions. There is only one solution to this problem: to make what one says more interesting. If the other participant is attempting to bring the subject of the discussion round to himself, it is usually an indication that the speaker has failed to reach the listener with his arguments. He has been unable to engage his interest. The intended aim of the conversation was not made clear. The arguments have not been understood.

If I as a layman wish to buy a car, and if the salesman indulges his love of technical detail in his sales talk, he should not be surprised if I repeatedly attempt to interrupt his flow of talk. Whether the engine is mounted obliquely or horizontally, how high the compression ratio is and what the transmission is like are matters which do not interest me. All I want, or think I want, is a vehicle priced in conformity with my income level which will convey me safely from one place to another.

This example illustrates a fundamental error which is committed again and again in discussions. One is so preoccupied with one's own ideas that one overlooks the possibility that the other person's interest might be centred on some completely different aspect. Clarification at the outset of the main preoccupation of those concerned makes it easier to establish the conversational style to be used and thus the form of argument.

CHAPTER V

Listening

It has already been indicated that a conversation consists of talking and listening. Talking is an art, but so is listening. It is possible to listen in an active way, and it is possible to listen passively. Active listening enlivens the conversation, while passive listening makes communication more difficult.

1 One can participate in a conversation without saying anything

A conversation is a reciprocal relationship. Monologues do not constitute a conversation. If one of the participants simply sits there while the other is talking and awaits his chance to start speaking again, a conversation cannot and will not develop. Listening is co-operation in the conversation. The listener should support the speaker during his talk, and should make it easier for him to express himself. He should help to carry the conversation along. Anyone talking expects that his words will have an effect. He expects to find agreement, reticence, scepticism or even rejection expressed by the person listening.

The listener must assist the talker by showing some reaction. He can express this inner sympathy with the speech of the other person by means of gestures, mimicry or by approving or disapproving interjections. A friendly nod of the head, a surprised "Oh", or a small interpolation such as "Interesting", show the talker that his arguments are reaching the listener. The listener can react simply by raising his eyebrows, wrinkling his brow, shrugging his shoulders, shaking his head or even uttering short, disapproving remarks such as "No", "Hardly". Approving remarks or gestures indicate that the speaker's arguments have been accepted and that he is proceeding on the right lines. If, however, he recognises a sceptical or disapproving reaction on the part of the listener, he will realise that so far his arguments have not got home. It would then be advisable for him to interrupt what he is saying and enquire into the cause of the sceptical or disapproving reaction; thus he will avoid wasting his time by continuing the same line of argument. How to react to contradiction will be discussed later.

2 One can listen without actually hearing

You know the type of person who sits languidly during a conversation with a slightly bored expression on his face, not taking in a word one says. People like this are incapable of taking in the argument or, more often, are not prepared to concern themselves with the other person. They are interested only in themselves and their own preconceived opinions. Such people are unfit to conduct a conversation. They must first learn to see beyond themselves.

PART TWO

The structure of a discussion

CHAPTER VI

Preparing for discussions

A knock at the door. The secretary enters.

"Mr. Evans is waiting outside and would like to talk to you."

"Mr. Evans? Who's he? What does he want?"

"I think Mr. Evans used to be a customer of ours. He didn't say what he wanted."

"Oh well, show him in."

Will anything come of this conversation? Everything so far seems to indicate that it will end in an inconclusive blah, blah.

How can I hold a conversation when I don't know who I am talking to, what is to be discussed, what the aim of this conversation is and what its implications will be?

Let us consider how a conversation should be constructed with a view to saving time and increasing the chances of success. Conversations must be prepared. But, you may say, it is not always possible to prepare a conversation. The majority of conversations occur unexpectedly. The secretary announces a visitor. Someone rings at the door, a friend, a business associate is waiting and would like to see me. A colleague calls me on the 'phone:

"Can I take up five minutes of your time?"

How can one be prepared for conversations like this?

I once asked friends, acquaintances and colleagues to make a note of the number of improvised discussions they had, for which they were given no opportunity to prepare themselves. The result of my investigations was conclusive. The cases in which real improvisation was necessary were so few that they can be completely disregarded.

I then asked the same people to ascertain how many discussions they entered without preparation because they found it inconvenient, considered it superfluous, or thought that they did not have sufficient time for preparation. It seemed that more than two-thirds of all discussions fell into this category.

The most common excuse for not preparing for talks is not having time. This is a superficial excuse. It conceals the fact that the person concerned is too easygoing to bother, or does not know how to set about the preparation. It is easy to prove the effort is worth while. Enter prepared and enter unprepared into discussions. Afterwards compare the results and the time expenditure. The additional time needed for unprepared talks – not to mention the extra nervous strain caused by being unprepared – is out of all proportion to the amount of time needed for systematic preparation.

There is an additional factor. If you approach someone who is well briefed when you yourself are unprepared, you are always in the less favourable position. The person who has prepared himself has the correct arguments at his finger tips, knows the right figures to two decimal points, knows the dates and the deadlines and you have no alternative but to take refuge in generalisations or to accept his information and admit to yourself that he is in control of the conversation.

Here is an example of how to prepare for a discussion, in a specific, practical case: "Good day, my name is Dauntless. I am sales manager of a firm manufacturing occasional furniture. We also produce other types of furniture. One of my duties is to maintain good relations with our large customers. Some time ago my order clerk informed me about the declining trend of business with the Saltain Furniture Store. At the time I decided to wait for a few weeks and see how the situation developed, but I have kept in regular contact with my clerk on this and now I have decided to discuss it with you."

The first stage in the preparations is to ask myself:

1 What do I actually wish to talk about?

I must be clear in my own mind what I wish to discuss with the firm. In this case the subject of the discussion is quite clearly the decline in turnover.

What should I know about the development of sales turnover in order to be able to discuss the subject?

First of all I must have detailed knowledge of sales to the Saltain Company in every line of furniture. For this purpose I ask my staff to prepare a sales analysis. The sales analysis must provide me with the trend of sales over the last three to four years; for seasonal articles, the effect of seasonal fluctuations must be clear. If turnover is distributed evenly over the whole year, I will need monthly figures.

Next I will need to know all the factors which influence turnover. How often has the customer been visited? Have differences of opinion arisen or have complaints been submitted by the customer? Have there been any changes in the customer's staff, for instance is there a different buyer? Has the competitive situation changed in any fundamental way, either with regard to the articles marketed by us or through the intensification of sales activities by competitive concerns?

I should not only investigate the turnover done with this customer, but should also compare it with our sales to other comparable customers. Can a general change of trend be detected? Is the turnover rate of the customer above or below the average for comparable customers? The information obtained in answering these questions will provide good material for use in the discussion.

Finally, the preparation must include a talk with the salesman who visits the Saltain company. Have his talks with employees of the Saltain company brought to light any circumstances which might exert an influence on turnover? What measures have been taken by the salesman to counteract the decline in turnover? What arguments has he produced and what has been the reaction to them? A comparison with his sales to other similar firms may provide useful background information for the discussion.

2 What do I expect from this discussion?

The next stage of preparation is working out the aim. Possible objectives in this case could be to increase the turnover again, to maintain the present turnover level, to slow down the decline in turnover or (in an extreme case) to reduce it intentionally. The first question in this respect must be: which objective is desirable in the company's interest? The second question: which objective is the most realistic?

There are many aspects of the question as to which objectives would be most desirable in the company's interest. Is our level of production capable of meeting higher levels of sales turnover? What effect would an increase in turnover have on the delivery deadline for this or that customer? Is it perhaps more in our interest to promote turnover to other stores? The interests of the company involve financial considerations. What is the customer's record of payment? On what terms of payment are sales effected? Is there a probability that an increase in turnover will necessitate an extension of credit? Could we accommodate this?

Another question which could arise is what selling aids would be necessary to bring about an increase in turnover? What level of advertising expenditure would be required? To what extent would additional customer services become necessary with an increase in turnover? Are we in a position to satisfy the anticipated requirements?

Price structure could also be affected by an increase in turnover. What further concessions would our present pricing level allow? Could we introduce new discount rates for increased turnover? Could we relieve the financial burden on our customer by providing some of the necessary finance and the increased storage facilities which would be needed? Could we supply some of the goods to the customer on a sale or return basis?

I must be absolutely clear about these and a number of other points before I can finally decide that an increase in turnover is the essential subject to be discussed. I must examine the other possible aims in the same light. Finally I must draw up a priority list of aims. The most desirable of these aims must be re-examined in terms of the specific requirements of my customers. I then firmly establish the aim of the forthcoming discussion by comparing what is desirable from my company's point of view with what can be realised from the point of view of the customer. Every subsequent stage in the preparation, as in the discussion itself, is worked out with this final objective in view.

Let us suppose that, after examining the matter, I reach the conclusion that I must have a discussion with the Saltain company for the purpose of maintaining the present turnover level. This automatically leads me to the next step in the preparation for the talks.

3 Who will I negotiate with?

My speculations about who to negotiate with must, as already mentioned, be based on the objective of the discussions. What I achieve in terms of turnover results from decisions made within the Saltain company. There are three possible ways in which these decisions are taken:

1 The company's top management determine the sales programme and the suppliers. The purchasing manager has a purely administrative function.
2 The purchasing manager decides on the goods to be bought and suppliers, following guidelines laid down and within the scope of a predetermined budget.
3 The sales department decides, on the basis of market information and its customer relationships, which goods should be purchased and which suppliers should be used.

In deciding who to approach with a view to holding discussions it is important to know who at the Saltain company makes the decisions which relate to my objectives. It is not always sound policy to negotiate with someone in as high a position as possible. It is more important that he should be competent to decide.

The sales department should have information on the duties and responsibilities of various key people in the purchasing firms. If so, the right man to talk to could be rapidly identified. Nevertheless it is advisable to check once again with a member of the sales force or with the customer firm whether the person in question or his reponsibilities have changed in any way. It can be embarrassing if the following situation in which I once found myself occurs.

For years I used to discuss certain business problems with one of my client's senior employees. When I attempted to reach him on one particular occasion, reception informed me coolly: "There is no person of this name in our company". I was introduced to his successor with the words: "This gentleman wanted to talk to a certain Mr. X, who doesn't work in this firm, but I think that you will be able to deal with the matter." The form of this introduction alone had already heaped unsuspected obstacles in my path.

In most cases, however, I will already be acquainted with the man I need to talk to. Nevertheless, it is expedient to refresh my memory about a person by looking through the last notes which I took or any other documents relating to him. What is his name? How old is he? What are his distinctive features? Does he enjoy meetings, is he approachable or is he reserved and difficult to establish contact with? Is he a hard-bargaining, down-to-earth negotiator for whom only the facts count, or is he the kind of man who likes to digress occasionally from the matter-of-fact subject of the negotiations? Are there subjects which he does not like to discuss, or others which he is always ready to talk about? Hobbies or other subjects to which he devotes much time?

I am the one who wants to obtain something from *him*, so it is my task to create the right atmosphere for the discussion.

At this point I must warn against a certain type of behaviour. To adapt oneself to one's opposite number does not mean fawning on him. Some time ago I had a customer who was aware of my particular interest in anything connected with the sea. So this client began every discussion with questions – and layman's questions into the bargain – on maritime topics. He was evidently hoping to please me by adopting this attitude, but he achieved exactly the opposite effect. One should not submerge one's own personality when entering into discussions with someone else. The essence of the approach is first and foremost to avoid anything which might create a strain. If I am not yet acquainted with the man I will be talking to, it will be much more difficult for me. Preparation for the discussion, in so far as it is a preparation for meeting him, will have to be more intensive. The minimum amount of information which I require includes the name of the man, his position in the company and when this is not obvious, a description of his actual duties. Any other available information about him may make preparation for the discussions easier. Approximately how old is he, how long has he been with the firm? What is known about his background? Can he be assigned to any particular recreational category such as tennis club, football, dancing? Even knowing his political attitudes can allow one to draw certain conclusions about him, at least as regards conversational taboos.

It is not always easy to obtain biographical information of this nature. In America there are commercial establishments devoted to "dissecting" personalities in commercial and public life, who then sell the results of their investigations. In Britain, a top-level businessman is likely to be in *"The Business Who's Who"*. Others may appear in a specialised "Who's Who" relating to finance, engineering or some other relevant profession or trade.

Obtaining information through secretaries' offices is not generally to be recommended. There are admittedly occasions when one may use this avenue – for instance when choosing a suitable anniversary or birthday present for a business associate; however, at other times it is to be avoided. I expect loyalty from my staff and I must work on the assumption that anyone I negotiate with expects a degree of loyalty from his staff. Just imagine the situation. Your secretary comes into your office and says: "You are having talks with Mr. Adamson tomorrow morning. His secretary just rang me and asked me what kind of person you are."

If all else fails, there is still the method by which you introduce yourself to the other person, giving items of information which you would like to know about him. In most cases the other party freely volunteers corresponding information about himself.

It is useful to draw up a short check-list of information about the other party, which should be obtained if possible before starting the discussion. Check-lists like this can easily be built up into small card-indexes, which one can supplement from time to time with personal impressions gained during actual discussions.

Before any future discussions which I or perhaps another member of the company will have to have with the same person, his main characteristics can readily be called to mind by consulting the card index.

4 Do I have the necessary technical knowledge?

When I have clarified for myself the subject of the discussions, their aim and the man I am likely to be talking to, I must ask myself the critical question: do I feel equal to the task? Do I possess the necessary specialist qualifications which will enable me to carry out my role effectively?

There is no need to repeat the points already made in Chapter III. The question to consider here is how can I compensate for specialised qualifications which I do not possess?

Should I consult specialized staff before the discussion? I have already indicated the dangers of this procedure. Should I include a specialist in the conversation? I shall refer again in a moment to the problems arising from such an action. Should I where necessary exclude certain specialized questions and leave them to be discussed by the relevant specialist?

I must decide on one course or another. I am manoeuvring myself into the weaker position if I only start to consider what I should do when technical questions which I am not competent to answer arise during the discussion. How much better is the impression if I am able to say with complete confidence: "I had foreseen the possibility that this question could arise and would suggest to you, since I do not feel myself qualified to deal with it, that we leave it to the experts on each side." This is much better than attempting to rescue myself by resorting to half-truths. Sooner or later I will have to admit my ignorance. By contrast the unhesitating admission of one's own limitations does not detract but rather adds to the status of a participant in a discussion. The concession "I have no idea about these things" contains the implicit statement: "I have a thorough knowledge of everything else I have been saying."

5 What should I be prepared for?

The question of whether I feel adequately qualified for a particular discussion leads automatically to the next question: "What arguments can I expect the other person to employ?"

The aim which I worked out in my preparation is to discuss the turnover level with my customer, with, let us say, the ultimate aim of maintaining the present rate of sales turnover. Are there perhaps questions and problems on the periphery of our sales activities which are directly or indirectly connected with the level of turnover? Slight overstepping of delivery deadlines which are usually regarded by the persons directly concerned as trivialities, and for this reason do not come to my attention at all, may be played up in the discussion. Slightly incorrect conduct of an employee, for instance an order clerk on the telephone or a delivery driver, may be resorted to as a substitute for real argument. Incorrect book entries which may arise after introduction of data processing methods can suddenly assume tremendous significance. Likewise the number, seriousness and method of attending to complaints may be exaggerated.

Arguments and problems presented in this form must first be subdivided into those which are justified and others which simply serve as a pretext. As a senior executive I ought to be informed about all problems of a serious nature. Nevertheless, I should make enquiries about such problems in all departments which have any sales relationships with the customer before the discussions with him take place. It is not sufficient for me to ask each department in turn: "Have there been any difficulties recently with the Saltain company?" What I ought to do, again with the aid of a check-list, is to ask specific questions.

Questions directed to the accounts department could, for example, include: "Is our invoicing up to date? Have there been any changes in bookings or any retrospective entries? Have any deadlines been overstepped? Have any customers' bills been recalculated? Have any conversations taken place regarding the calculation of discounts? When were the accounts last balanced and what was the result?"

If there are serious problems which I expect to be raised in the discussion, I should work out beforehand how I intend to handle them. On the other hand, "pretext" arguments usually take the form of standard objections, recurring with almost every customer. Every good salesman knows that his customer has a dozen or so defensive arguments which are constantly repeated, even if they are varied in emphasis. Prepare yourself for these standard objections by being forearmed with corresponding counter-arguments. One is then continually master of the situation and can be sure of being consistent in argument.

If the favourite topic of incorrect accounts entries on changing over to data processing is mentioned, I immediately place myself in the weaker position if I react with surprise and tell the customer that I know nothing about this, but that I will have the matter looked into immediately and that he will then no doubt receive a satisfactory answer from us. A far better impression is given if I immediately admit: "You are absolutely correct. We are aware of these difficulties and it is a matter of extreme regret to us that a number of incorrect accounts entries have arisen during the transition period. Indeed we have already apologised to you for it. The fault which caused these incorrect entries has, however, been located and rectified. We are taking all possible steps to ensure that such errors do not occur again." Such candour disarms the other person. Today everybody realises that a change-over from manual accounting to a data processing system means that a few problems will arise in the transition period. It is, however, not possible to alter anything which has already happened. It is far more to the point to make a statement about the avoidance of similar errors in the future.

The professional experience of the man you will be talking to can influence the questions which may arise. The furniture buyer in the Saltain company has a narrower view of the business relations between our companies than for instance the director in charge of all buying; he again has a less broad view than the managing director. The higher the other party is in the company, the broader will be the range of questions which I must be prepared to deal with.

Reduced to a common denominator: to the furniture buyer I am a salesman of furniture; to the head of the purchasing department I am a representative of the sales department; to the managing director I represent my company. I must take this into account when preparing for a discussion.

6 How much time do I have available for the discussion?

An important point in my preparation is deciding how much time I should set aside for the discussion. This decision must be made on the basis of the following facts. A systematic discussion demands the concentration of those involved. Concentration is a function of time. If we designate the capacity for concentration at the start of the discussion as zero, this concentration increases sharply at the beginning of the discussion until it reaches a maximum. It remains at this peak for a short period, then starts to decline gradually and then more rapidly as the discussion goes on, until it reaches zero once more. The level of concentration may even drop below the zero point. Continuing the discussion beyond this point will only meet with reluctance on the part of the listener. It is therefore senseless to prolong a discussion over an indefinite period of time. Preparation for the discussion must include choosing the most favourable time-period and also deciding on the distribution of the subject matter over this period.

The first and fundamental determinant for length of conversation is one's own capacity for concentration. If I have to conduct discussions frequently, I must examine myself critically to determine how long I can concentrate. In rhetoric there is a well-known rule of thumb: "Anything may be discussed, but not for more than 70 minutes."

In principle a discussion should not last more than one hour. This is a long time, from which one can extract a great deal if the discussion is held in a methodical way.

Not only my own capacity for concentration, but also that of the other party plays an important role. If I am already acquainted with him, I should have a good idea of his capacity for concentration. Flagging concentration on the part of the participants in a

C

discussion becomes evident in the increasing readiness of those concerned to deviate from the subject under discussion and to chat about inconsequential matters, also in the difficulty they have in returning to the subject under discussion or in focusing the other person's attention on it again.

Of course, the subject itself and one's familiarity with it play a part in determining one's capacity for concentration. It is moreover possible to increase one's concentration and that of the person one is talking to by the style of speaking one employs.

Where one is dealing with a person one doesn't know, information obtained in advance about him allows certain conclusions to be drawn about his capacity for concentration. This is particularly so when the personal information I have at my disposal allows me to draw comparisons with people I already know. Otherwise I must enter the discussion with an experimental attitude and watch carefully for the point in the discussions when signs of fatigue begin to appear.

Concentration should, of course, never be allowed to drop below the zero level, for a discussion which is drawn out beyond this point provokes a reaction of refusal and in certain circumstances a physical reluctance to continue. The eventual result of the discussion is thereby seriously impaired.

It is always in one's interest to conclude a discussion at the peak of one's own concentration. However, there are dangers even here and a certain type of bad salesman comes to mind. He hopes to succeed quickly by applying coercive tactics. He simply does not recognise that the customer has already switched off mentally and is only giving reflex answers in the form of yes and no. Whether the sale will eventually take place, or whether the customer departs without the business having been transacted, this talk has achieved one definite result. It is most unlikely that the customer will return. He feels he has been molested by this excessive persistence.

One should enquire about the length of time allotted for the discussion when making the initial appointment. Today this is usual both in commercial and private life; it is accepted practice to fix the duration of the conversation in advance. This enables the two parties concerned to plan their timetables, and also makes the planning of the conversation and its conclusion easier.

If I have agreed upon a one-hour discussion, I can end it after exactly one hour without being impolite. I no longer need, as previously, to look at my watch, first timidly and then with increasing ostentation, in order to make it clear to the other man that I wish to conclude or that there are other claims on my time. Nor do I need to instruct my secretary to enter after an hour has elapsed and announce that the chairman would like to speak to me!

Establishing the length of time for the discussion also makes it possible for me to choose the most favourable time of day. One's ability to conduct discussions with concentration and effectiveness varies throughout the day. Many people like to begin their day's work with negotiations, others prefer to round off their working day with them. I have known colleagues in other departments whom it was most advisable to approach directly after lunch, while others found conversation at this time of the day an intolerable annoyance. The choice of the correct time of day is closely related to fixing the duration of a discussion.

7 Wouldn't it be better to have another person present?

Many years ago I had the following experience. One of my customers came to see me to discuss his account. At the appointed time my secretary announced: "Five gentlemen have arrived who would like to speak to you. They are from Swindle & Company." The men were shown in. They proved to be made up of the following people: the proprietor of the firm, his son who was still engaged in his studies at the time and not yet active in the firm, the head of the accounts department, the tax adviser and the company lawyer. Should I let myself in for this talk? Not that I was apprehensive about being outnumbered 1 : 5 or that I feared there were dishonest motives behind this mustering of staff. My thoughts were quite different: Why – excluding the son, who has been brought along for training purposes – is the man I am supposed to be talking to accompanied by the head of his accounts department, his tax adviser and his lawyer? Without doubt he expects that specialised questions will arise in this discussion – in fact matters relating to law and tax – which he does not feel sufficiently confident to handle.

The next question is whether I feel confident to handle the matters which he obviously expects to arise. In this instance I brought in the head of our legal department. This move soon proved justified. For tax reasons my customer was planning certain changes which would have considerable effect on our commercial relationship. I would not have been able to cope with this situation on my own.

The head of the legal department could of course have been brought in at a later point, that is the point at which the legal and fiscal questions actually arose in the discussion. This would have had the disadvantage that he would not have known all the background information, the motives and reasons for the intended changes. The discussion would then have been delayed by numerous repetitions and explanations. By participating from the very beginning, he was able to discuss the specialised questions arising, with a complete understanding of their context.

A discussion among several people raises its own type of problem. We shall be returning to this subject in the third section of the book. None the less, it will prove necessary again and again for several people to take part in a discussion when the subject at issue is of a very complex nature.

If problems from various specialised fields are touched upon in a discussion, there is a danger that misunderstandings may arise when reports of the negotiations are passed on to the departments concerned. One must therefore find out where the activities of other departments fall within the scope of the intended negotiations and whether these departments should participate directly. Often this is a matter which I cannot decide on my own. The other departments must themselves be consulted.

If it is decided in advance that a third person or a number of people from one's own company should take part in the negotiations, the other party should automatically be informed of this intention and if necessary his agreement obtained. He will thus have the opportunity to bring similar specialist aides and make similar preparations. If he expressly requests a *tête-à-tête*, then I should comply with his wishes, unless this is against the interests of my company.

8 A "crib" is not a sign of uncertainty

The penultimate question in the preparation for talks is what documents will be necessary?

You are, of course, familiar with the usual opening ceremonies. The man in question arrives. He or his underlings drag a briefcase or rather a chest filled to bursting point with documents into the conference room. A searching glance: where can I hang my coat, where can I spread everything out? The briefcase is opened. A multitude of notebooks, files, loose sheets and documents stapled together come into view. Finally a notebook bound in crocodile skin is produced and opened. Right, the discussion can begin.

It is also part of the ensuing ceremony that from time to time, usually when the visitor is faced with a critical situation, he starts searching wildly for some specific document among the stack of material he has brought with him. Naturally the required item is not found. Of course it is there somewhere. He was just looking at it before he set off. Unfortunately it seems to have disappeared at the very time it is needed.

These heaps of documents betray inadequate preparation for the discussion. The person concerned had leafed through every single sheet at home an hour or two before arriving for the talks. He wanted to be prepared as well as possible for any question which might arise. Every single document had a contribution to make. As a result he is not prepared for anything at all.

First let us establish a basic axiom: documents impede the discussion, they do not help it along. A briefcase full of sheets of paper, letters, photocopies, etc., brought along by one of the negotiators has an alarming effect on the other participant. What should *he* have brought? What will the other man be conjuring up next out of his little box?

This is not the only aspect to be considered. Papers are a source of confusion, especially if the documents in question are not the product of one's own initiative or if one has not previously studied them thoroughly. Anyone who uses documents drawn up by a colleague or member of staff must take into account that they may have been produced from different background information. Any attempt to interpret written statements on the basis of different background information not infrequently leads to confusion and even error.

By this I do not mean that written documents are superfluous in a discussion. Quite the opposite. Many business negotiations could not be conducted at all without them. There are, however, two fundamental principles which must be observed. First the documents must be very closely related to one's own mental preparation for the negotiations. They must be a logical development of this preparation. Second, less is more. The written document itself is not the essence of the discussion, but should rather assist the negotiators at certain stages to conduct the talks as purposefully as possible.

The most important written document is the plan for the discussion. Yes, that is quite correct. The arrangement of the discussion, the questions which it is essential to clarify or resolve during the talks and the so-called "thread" should always be sketched out in writing.

Haven't you ever had quite a lengthy discussion, and only after it was over did all those things occur to you which you really ought to have discussed but in fact did not? This situation must be avoided at all costs. The subject of the discussion, its ultimate goal and the stages by means of which one intends to arrive at this goal should all be noted down. It is surprising how many new points occur to you if you just take the trouble to set down on paper the various propositions to be treated in the forthcoming talks.

A plan for a discussion is nevertheless not to be regarded as a strict formula admitting of no deviation. It is purely and simply an aid. It enables us, without great mental exertion, to recover and return to the original object and aim of the discussion should digressions occur.

The written documents must obviously include any which form

an integral part of the discussions. If it is intended to discuss the contents of a letter, the verbatim text must be at hand. A contract can only be interpreted or discussed on the basis of the original text. However, there are also written documents which I need only to support my own statements – a survey of turnover trends, for instance, either in the form of figures or graphs or a compilation of data which are relevant to my arguments, even including drawings and photographs.

Finally I must consider documents which do not perhaps have any great significance in the discussion itself, but which might help the other person to assimilate and consider the subject under discussion, or which could be agreed upon as a suitable subject for further talks. These might include for instance design drawings, descriptions of certain processes, operating instructions and solvency calculations. Any material I prepare for the other participant must be comprehensible to him. Specialised statements should be translated into terms which are meaningful to him.

Once I have decided what written documents will be essential for the talks, I must give each a reference number and coordinate these reference numbers with the draft layout I have drawn up for the discussion. This somewhat crude but nevertheless effective aid will make it easier for me to be able to place the correct documents on the table at the appropriate moment, without having to interrupt the flow of conversation by a protracted search. Written documents are not there simply to be read out. Reading aloud is always boring for adults. It becomes quite impossible when the person who goes to the lengths of quoting from his written documentation also experiences difficulty with the actual reading of the text. Or if the section he wishes to quote expresses the complete opposite of what it was intended to prove.

In summarising, I should like to repeat: written documents are permissible when absolutely essential. Under no circumstances, however, should they have a disruptive effect on the discussion.

9 How do I create the right atmosphere?

When I have completely thought through all aspects of the

proposed discussion, and have made the necessary specialised and technical preparations, I should finally consider the circumstances and atmosphere. These can have a decisive influence on the result. I must therefore consider how I can contribute towards creating a favourable atmosphere.

Where and in what conditions should the discussion take place? Is there anything the other man is particularly sensitive about? Are technical aids required for the talks? Are there any special factors which I must take into account with regard to the other person, such as illnesses or other handicaps? What can I do to reduce any inhibitions which the other man may have? Inhibitions should be expected when there are considerable social or educational differences between the participants in talks. They can also arise when the relationship between the persons concerned is strained, for whatever reasons, by external or even personal differences.

Finally, much thought must be given to the introduction to the discussion. We shall return to this subject in the next chapter. For the moment let it be mentioned that establishing a close personal relationship is an essential part of preparation for a discussion.

CHAPTER VII

Where should the discussion take place?

I have just indicated that the circumstances in which a discussion takes place can have a decisive effect on the atmosphere. Should I invite the other person to come to me, should I visit him, should I suggest that the discussions are held in an informal atmosphere?

For this there is a rule of thumb in business practice: the person who wants something should visit the person from whom he hopes to obtain it.

This is really an over-simplification. One must be aware of the advantages and disadvantages of the various alternatives. The venue for the discussion should then be suggested, taking these factors into account, as well as the topic for discussion and the aim of the talks. Remember also that the choice of location is not a decision which rests exclusively with you. Although it is unacceptable in social life, in the business world it is acceptable to invite oneself. To start off a request for an appointment with the words: "I should like very much to pay you a visit in the course of the next few days" would by no means be offensive. Yet to invite someone to one's own office for talks has a rather official ring and seems like something in the nature of a "summons". Invitations to one's own office should therefore be presented in the form of a suggestion, to make it easier for the other person to agree.

1 Lord and master within one's own four walls

If a discussion takes place in my own office, I am master of the house and host. As such I have all the duties but also all the rights attaching to this position, in business as well as in social life. This means above all that I must create the necessary conditions to ensure a smooth and pleasant round of talks.

First and foremost, I must attend to the welfare of my guest. The first requirement is to ensure that he finds his way to me without a hitch. How pleasant it is when you enter a strange firm and right at the entrance you are greeted by your name: "Ah, yes, of course, Mr. Brown, you are expected, if you would accompany me upstairs" or "Miss Harrison, the secretary, will take you upstairs immediately." The very opposite to this is the grumbling doorman who asks you: "Who do you want to see? Have you got an appointment? Wait a minute, I'll see if Mr. X has time to talk to you." Then you stand around in a draughty entrance or slightly forlorn in a large reception hall, bereft amongst the comings and goings of preoccupied employees. Finally, the announcement issues from a glass booth: "You there, go up to Mr. X. Go to the third floor, turn right down the corridor, on the left-hand side you will find room 204. First report to room 205. The secretary there will tell you when you can go in to Mr. X."

Not only is the smooth reception of a guest important; the host must also be ready to greet his guest at the appointed time. If I have made an appointment to see someone at 10 o'clock, I must be there to receive him at 10 and not at one minute past. This is not being excessively fastidious, it is merely polite. No telephone conversation can be so important, no signature can be so indispensable that the guest must be kept waiting.

A business discussion is a form of work; so the host is obliged to create suitable working conditions for his guest. Any guest who is obliged to deposit his briefcase and most of his papers on the floor, or for whom the host laboriously clears a small corner of his desk so that at least he has somewhere to put his notebook, is a very bad host. A sufficiently large conference table is essential for a discussion during which it may be necessary to refer to documents. However, where the need for documents is not anticipated, a large conference table might have an undesirable effect, diminishing the contact between persons. A change of venue during the discussion from conference table to slightly more intimate surroundings can be valuable.

Consideration must also be given to technical aids, starting with relatively trivial things. Is there any notepaper, a pencil or ball-point pen within reach should the guest have need of them? How embarrassing it is if he asks for paper or writing materials and the host must first set in motion an entire requisitioning system.

If foreign language documents are introduced into the discussion, translation facilities must be available. Don't employ your own frequently inadequate linguistic knowledge for translation purposes. A translator has the advantage of greater credibility. If it is considered necessary for points of agreement to be recorded during the discussion, it is expedient to have a tape-recorder in readiness.

In discussions on technical subjects it may be necessary to have a blackboard, projector or display screen and light pen to illustrate a point which has been raised without disturbing the flow of the discussion. If a number of people are taking part in the talks on each side, then one must at least be prepared for the possibility that the main visitor may wish to withdraw to confer among his own colleagues. With this in view one should ensure that a suitable adjoining room is available and that a typist is available too.

If it is proposed to extend the discussion over a considerable period of time, one must give some thought to how the time can be broken up, so giving the participants a chance to regenerate the capacity for concentration.

Interposing a short interval from time to time is not the best way of achieving this. Such pauses generally mean only a continuation of the conversation from a different approach. One must provide genuine diversion and relaxation. Perhaps a short tour of some section of the works, the display of a new piece of equipment to divert the attention for a while to a completely different topic or a short stroll outside; these are all methods which have proved consistently successful. An important part in protracted discussions is also played by the necessary "facilities". Remember to inform your guests at the beginning of the first break where they can "freshen up".

Whether and to what extent I must entertain anyone I am holding discussions with is a matter of tact. In principle, there is of course no obligation to entertain my business guest. Cigarettes and non-alcoholic refreshment should be within easy reach. If I know that my guest has come a long way, I should see to it that coffee or tea is available. Alcoholic drinks are inappropriate and should not be offered during business negotiations. If these extend over a mealtime and a meal is served, an aperitif is suitable to relax both host and guest, but alcohol during the meal is inadvisable. It will make some of the participants sleepy during the subsequent talks.

The host must not only ensure that all due formalities are observed in the talks, it is also his responsibility to see that they are successful. He must initiate the discussion. He must see to it that the necessary contact is established. He must also be capable of smoothing over difficult situations which arise, particularly the removal of misunderstandings. Last but not least he must ensure that the aim of the discussions is achieved.

This extensive list of duties attendant upon the host is compensated for by the unquestionable advantages of being master in one's own house. It is the equivalent of a home match. One is working in familiar surroundings. I pick up the telephone, push a button and in my own firm I can immediately obtain any information I require. My opponent, on the other hand, has to rely on his preparation or any help I care to offer him. The host not only has the duty but also possesses the right to open the discussion. This right offers him the possibility of taking the initiative, making suggestions and "leading" the discussion. Leading does not mean that he should dominate it. Leading should be understood here in the sense of guiding.

One of the most important obligations of the host is to provide an undisturbed atmosphere in which the discussions can take place. They should not be interrupted, either by telephone messages or by the notorious signatures which have to be appended to various documents from time to time or by urgent instructions issued to secretaries or assistants. Every interruption means that contact is disrupted and it is almost necessary to go back to the start: "Where were we when we left off?" Trains of thought must be built up all over again.

Finally, it is left to the host's initiative to conclude the talks or at least to give indications that the discussion should be drawing to a close. This is his privilege.

2 A visit can be used to express deference

Have you ever summoned an employee to your office on his 25th anniversary with the company in order to congratulate him on his service? Surely not. You went to him. You went to see him at his place of work or even perhaps at home. Why did you do that? Your visit was meant to pay him a special compliment. The employee tells his friends and acquaintances: "The boss came to see me in person."

Take another situation. The door of your office opens and the chairman of the Board of Directors enters. You naturally regard this as a special form of recognition and your attitude is to your guest's advantage. Most people would prefer to talk to someone who enhances their status with a visit.

The announcement of this visit is probably expressed in the form of a request: "I should like to pay you a visit sometime," or "Might I drop in and see you during the next few days" or "To save you any inconvenience, I will be glad to visit you." Can you imagine the announcement of an intended visit being expressed like this: "Please make arrangements for me to visit you tomorrow morning at 10 o'clock!" This may be how an ill-mannered receiver in bankruptcy would address a common debtor, but it is obviously not the approach normally adopted. I can imply a great deal by the way in which I express my desire to visit someone else.

3 The significance of the lunch table

It is sometimes said that the most successful transactions are concluded not at the office desk but at the lunch table. This may well be so, and one important reason is that an outside hotel or restaurant represents neutral ground. It is more relaxing than the office of either party. Progress in discussions can be swifter when both parties feel free from the formality of their normal work surroundings.

The lunch table also has a conciliatory effect. A meal together can act as a catalyst. Common love of good food and drink makes it easier to see that the other person is not as bad as one thought.

4 A discussion cannot be held at any old time or place

Have you ever attempted to hold a discussion with a business associate at half past twelve at night in a draughty railway station, just as his train was departing, leaving you standing on the platform? What was the result? Surely you didn't even attempt such a thing? How could one ever come to be talking business in such circumstances? This is an extreme example. However, the simple realisation that each discussion needs its own atmosphere is often overlooked.

The subject and aim of the discussion should play a decisive part in determining the conditions under which it should be held. If I wish to announce the termination of a business relationship or to submit a serious complaint, then I must carry this out at my own offices. Imagine the situation where a serious disagreement occurs during talks held in my business associate's office. As master of the house he has the right to discontinue the talks at any point he wishes, to show me the door and forbid me to visit him again. Admittedly in the same situation I cannot prevent my guest from perhaps breaking off the discussion and leaving of his own accord. None the less, there is a difference between leaving talks of your own accord and being shown the door during talks held at someone else's premises.

I always try to conduct contract negotiations, which frequently necessitate the attendance of specialist staff, at my own offices. On the other hand, if I am trying to obtain concessions from the other person, if I wish to request something from him or if I have to apologise for errors and oversights on the part of my firm, it is better to visit him at his offices. For talks which involve an element of strain a neutral atmosphere is recommended.

The time of day chosen should be appropriate both to the

subject and the intention behind the discussion. For instance I would not engage in credit negotiations between 11 a.m. and 1 p.m. This happens to be the busiest period of the day in a bank or finance house. I would have to take into account that the person I was approaching would be constantly preoccupied with many other things during our conversation. Moreover, people react in very different ways at different times. There are certain people who are "all there" as soon as they open their eyes. On the other hand there are the "morning grumblers" who must be allowed three to four hours' grace before one can even address a word to them. The choice of the correct time and suitable surroundings can be of decisive importance for the outcome of a discussion.

CHAPTER VIII

The "first impression"

First impressions are important when two people meet. They can captivate, like "love at first sight", or provoke defensive reactions. If the man one is dealing with makes a favourable first impression, one does not regard him or listen to him so critically. If the first impression is unfavourable, every word and every gesture may be closely analysed. The slightest indiscretion is only too readily taken as confirmation of the first unfavourable impression.

It will be obvious that first impressions can be extremely dangerous, particularly if one's main preoccupation during the discussion is to confirm them. What exactly is a first impression?

1 "I, with my knowledge of human nature . . ."

Have you ever met anyone who admitted that he had no intuitive knowledge of his fellow men? Knowledge of people is as essential in modern life as a clean handkerchief, well-brushed teeth or good digestion.

Where does knowledge of one's fellow man spring from?

"Knowledge of one's fellow man is based on experience," I was once told during a seminar. Experience is the sum total of all the setbacks encountered during one's life. It is generally based on a series of negative perceptions. The knowledge that one will be burned by a hot oven is based on the fact that at some time or other, perhaps during childhood, one has touched a hot oven.

Again and again one sees that this so-called knowledge of fellow man is evolved more from negative than from positive reactions. In a sense it can be regarded as a statistical mean value. When I drive on the motorway I am repeatedly annoyed by people who drive a certain type of car. This repeated experience leads me to believe that people who have this type of car are generally bad drivers. This generalisation becomes an item in my total "knowledge of people". If someone tells me that he drives this particular type of vehicle, I automatically assume that I am dealing with a lout. I have added one more specimen to my gallery of human types. Height, build, hair colour, physical features, all these are points on which assessment of human nature is based. Take care! This kind of judgement is dominated by emotional considerations. Therefore it provokes emotional reactions.

2 Punctuality is the politeness of kings

Among the numerous systems for personality development, there exists in America a school of thought which runs on the following lines: Never be on time; if you are unpunctual all the attention will be focused on you. Even if this attention has a negative basis, it is nevertheless increased attention. Unpunctuality always gives you the opportunity of bringing the conversation round to yourself. You also have the chance to take the lead in the conversation by the way in which you present your excuses for being late.

A meeting starting like this could take the following form: "I'm terribly sorry for being slightly late. Good heavens, almost 15 minutes. But I'm sure you'll understand, an urgent call came through from Tokyo and one can't simply walk out on new business. But we'll soon make up the 15 minutes. I don't think we should concern ourselves too much with points, 1, 3 and 5. I suggest that to save time we should start with point 2. On this point I think that . . ."

My opinion about punctuality is quite different! It can provide an important clue to personality. Have you ever noticed in your firm, in your circle of friends, at the annual general meeting of the Chamber of Commerce, etc., that it is always the same people who cannot manage to keep an appointment? It is always these particular people who are detained at the very last moment by an important telephone conversation, an unexpected visitor whom one would have liked to put off, of course, and so on. And it just happens that these same people are the ones who hand in their turnover statements etc. at 11 instead of 10 o'clock and whose post arrives in the dispatch department half an hour after the service has closed. One is quite justified in drawing certain conclusions about personalities, not on the basis of punctuality but rather of unpunctuality.

I have already mentioned that it is one of the duties of a host to receive his guest at the appointed time. However, the guest also has an obligation to arrive punctually. He must allow for the fact that the traffic is very heavy at certain times of the day, that the traffic lights might all be against him.

The next time you have to visit a client, arrange things so that you arrive at his offices five to ten minutes before the appointed time. Take advantage of these five or ten minutes to take a short stroll round the office block or to have a look in a few shop windows. After this go in and have your discussion. You will be surprised at the effect which these five to ten minutes have had. You are relaxed, you have increased confidence, you radiate calmness and composure. If on the other hand you arrive ten minutes late and with a bad conscience then you are the very personification of agitation, uncertainty, distractedness, nervousness and awkwardness. The first words you utter have to be an apology. Right at the beginning you have imparted a negative tone to the entire discussion.

3 There can be no accounting for tastes

Do you remember? A few years ago when it became fashionable for young people of both sexes to wear their hair long, our connoisseurs of human nature were quick off the mark with pertinent associations of ideas. Long hair, that means rebellion against traditional social standards. Anyone who had long hair smoked hashish and voted for radical left-wing parties. The long-hairs met with the rejection of society. Today, however, we are completely accustomed to their appearance. We have learnt to realise that tastes quite simply differ. Young people of all social levels and types, even some older people, adopted this fashion. Today no one asks whether hair is short or long, only whether it is well cared for or not. But even the idea "well cared-for" is a relative concept. Comparison of the amount of time spent on personal hygiene and on looking after one's car shows this.

An inclination to wear modern clothing is by no means the sign of an extravagant nature. Once again the decisive factor is not the audacity of fashion but rather the standard of personal grooming. It is not admissible to claim that someone will be more or less efficient when wearing a lace shirt as against a traditional poplin shirt. What is more valid, however, is the conclusion that someone who neglects his appearance will also be careless in his work.

There are, nevertheless, upper and lower sartorial limits which should be observed out of consideration for those one is negotiating with. It is more a matter of style than taste. One may justifiably draw the conclusion that a person unwilling to make concessions in this regard will scarcely be inclined to do so in other matters.

4 "My father put me on the right track . . ."

"My father put me on the right track. He warned me to be careful about red-heads, hunchbacks and people who deny having any principles." Not very long ago I heard this sentiment expressed by an employee. The man in question was not 18 or 20 years old but over 50. Naturally he had considerable knowledge of his fellow men, based on these inherited guidelines.

Much of what we regard as innate knowledge of our fellow men is the product of our education. We grow up in certain surroundings – within a certain social class which determines our idea of a "normal person". Anyone who deviates from this standard is simply regarded as "different". In this case "different" means that on the basis of our experience we will never get on with this type of person. He causes difficulties for us and is therefore suspect.

What we consider knowledge of other people is often no more than prejudice. A friend of mine is always suspicious of people who like hybrid tea roses. Why? His first flame, who left him in the lurch, was very fond of hybrid tea roses.

Let us be warned against allowing our attitude towards others to be conditioned by prejudice. It can diminish the freedom of the discussion and even limit our own freedom.

5 Confidence should not be confused with arrogance

Two concepts which are frequently confused by pseudo-connoisseurs of human nature are confidence and arrogance. Naturally these two characteristics are very closely related. The point where confidence ends and arrogance begins is a matter of subjective assessment. A self-assured manner arises from a thorough understanding and mastery of the rules of combat that are regarded as acceptable in social intercourse. Permissible modes of conduct in society have changed in recent years. The concept of authority among the younger generation is quite different from that of older people. The traditional concept of authority is one which derives from an official position. Therefore anyone who judges relationships of authority according to traditional standards will regard someone who makes it clear that he does not consider official rank as synonymous with authority as presumptuous and arrogant. The latter's basis for assessing authority is totally different. In carrying out dealings with him I must simply accept the fact that his fundamental concepts are different, and that he has a right to hold them.

CHAPTER IX

The greeting

The greeting is the first direct and personal contact which occurs between the participants in a discussion. It signals the actual start of the discussion. The first words exchanged in greeting can be decisive for the atmosphere and the course of the entire discussion.

1 Who may I say is calling?

It is important that there is complete clarity from the start as to the identity of each person involved. At the very least both participants must be informed of the name and function of the other person. As a visitor, it will be necessary to announce oneself: to the doorman, the floor porter, reception or the secretary of the person one is visiting. This announcement can either be made orally or by handing over a visiting card. In this latter case the name of the visitor and not of his company should predominate. If spoken, one should pronounce one's name clearly and precisely, so that it is passed on correctly. If it is an unusual name or difficult to pronounce, spell it out letter by letter.

When announcing oneself orally, it is not usual to give one's title or official function. It is quite adequate to say: "My name is Benson from the Heavyweight Company. I have an appointment at 10 o'clock with Mr. Lightfoot (or the head of your purchasing department or your managing director)." On the other hand one ought to have a visiting card to facilitate this procedure. The information on the card should, in order of emphasis, be the name of the visitor, the name of the company, and one's job function. A visiting card is not an advertising medium, only an aid for the other person to recognise the visitor, and adopt an appropriate attitude towards him. If the visitor has already announced himself in this fashion, he does not need to repeat his name when he is greeted by his host. The host for his part can assume that the visitor is already acquainted with *his* name.

2 "Mr. . . . what was your name?"

The purpose of announcing oneself is to provide a mutual acquaintance with the names of the host and his visitor. The name must be pronounced clearly enough at the greeting stage, so that the other person can repeat it correctly and with confidence. If difficulties in pronunciation arise, these should be cleared up immediately.

One frequently finds that the pronunciation of a name varies considerably, especially if the name is of foreign origin. For example, the pronunciation used by some descendants of emigrant Huguenot families is sometimes identical to the written language, while others still pronounce their name in the French manner. Before pronouncing a name, it is worth making sure of the correct pronunciation while the introductions are still being effected. It is by no means impolite to greet your guest with the words: "Good morning Mr. Cockburn – I hope I have pronounced your name correctly?" This is better than to subject the guest to the imposition of hearing his name repeatedly pronounced in a mutilated way. The question: "I'm afraid I didn't quite catch your name when we were introduced, what did you say it was?" is better than mumbling the other person's name whenever it is necessary to address him directly in the course of the discussion. The guest will be sure to notice if the host has got it wrong or if he is vague.

If there has been any change in the selection of participants since the arrangements were made, the other party must be informed. For instance, the host might say: "You had an appointment with Mr. Samson but Mr. Samson is ill. He didn't come into work this morning. My name is Delilahman. My work is associated very closely with that of Mr. Samson. He has given me all the relevant information about the subject to be discussed."

3 We don't always shake hands these days

What is the significance of hand contact? Is the shaking of hands intended to create a specially cordial atmosphere? This can hardly be the case. Even wrestlers and boxers shake hands before they start their contest. Is it perhaps a symbolic gesture which says that they will remain friends no matter what happens? The ritual of shaking hands is on the wane but it is important that a greeting be exchanged at the start of a discussion. The specific form that this greeting takes is of secondary importance. Usually the host takes a few steps forward to greet his guest and proffers his hand. It is not, however, impolite if he does not do this. Each guest must be given individual attention and a few words of greeting, whether or not there is a handshake.

4 Social formalities must be observed in the business world

Social formalities must be observed when a meeting takes place. The host must offer his guest somewhere to sit. He must only sit down when the guest is already seated. If the host does not offer his guest somewhere to sit, the guest has the right to exercise his initiative and occupy the place nearest to his host. After the greeting has taken place and both persons are seated, the guest must wait for his host to make the opening remarks in the discussion. The guest may only take this initiative if his host expresses, by conclusive gestures, that he does not wish to exercise this right himself.

If a number of people are taking part in a discussion, they must become acquainted with each other before the start of the talks. It is the duty of the host to effect the introductions and to explain the functions or reasons which have made it necessary for additional people to be present. If the guest has brought along additional participants, it is his duty to explain their presence and to introduce them accordingly.

CHAPTER X

Contact

Every discussion must be built up on contact. What does this mean? What significance does contact have for the conversation?

It is the purpose of contact to establish a bond between those about to engage in a discussion. This bond must sustain the burden of the discussion. The establishment of contact has sometimes been described as a warming-up period, acclimatisation, or simply "sizing up".

The contact phase is decisive but it does not need a great deal of time. A contact talk does not even need to last ten minutes. A word, a sentence, perhaps a gesture can create contact. Generally speaking it is easier and quicker to establish contact between smokers than between non-smokers. The offering of a cigarette or a light, leaning over towards each other and the temporary concentration on the lighting of cigarettes, the words exchanged about smoking itself, or the brand of cigarettes, all of these generate a certain feeling of intimacy. The same also applies to the offering of drinks. Serving up coffee or tea or pouring out refreshing drinks, creates the same feeling of rapport as the offering of cigarettes.

1 Contact comes from "contangere"

The need for a contact phase at the beginning of the discussion arises from the fact that the participants have just left behind different preoccupations in order to take part in this discussion. The host was involved with another problem before his guest arrived. The guest, who may have come by car, has been concentrating on the traffic. Mentally he may be still preoccupied with it. It is important to bring all the participants in the discussion on to the same wavelength. This contact phase is designed to bring the conversation gradually to the actual subject of the discussion by first talking about topics of common interest.

The word contact is derived from the Latin *contangere*. *Contangere* means to touch. Points of contact are to be sought between the various persons: mutual interests or indeed anything in common which would create a spirit of community. What subject should I choose to establish this contact? This is discussed more fully later, but there are three subjects which are generally considered unsuitable for contact talks: ideological questions, illnesses and party-political matters!

2 Who is responsible for establishing contact?

Every participant in the talks should be interested in seeing that the discussion takes place in the best possible atmosphere. The primary responsibility for a good atmosphere, as has already been mentioned, rests with the host. It is his task to start off the talks and to establish a bond between the other person or persons. The guest should not take the initiative in establishing contact. He ought to assume that the host has prepared himself for this discussion, and has also given thought to how he would like to start it off. It is impolite, and does not help to create a good atmosphere, to deprive the host of his opportunity. At the same time, the host must be conscious of his obligations to create a suitable atmosphere. It is part of his preparation for the talks to consider how contact is to be established.

It is often said that there are people who are good at establishing contact and others who are not, and that those who are good at establishing contact are therefore superior in a business discussion. There is an element of truth in this assertion. However, this kind of deficiency can be remedied. By working on oneself and by thorough preparation it is possible to compensate to a great extent for any deficiency, which is frequently based on a feeling of inadequacy.

Establishing contact should always involve suitable preparation.

As someone who finds it easy to establish contact I cannot rely entirely on my ability, thinking "Let him come along. Something will occur to me." If he is sitting opposite me, then usually nothing occurs to me other than everyday questions about his journey or the weather. If I have dealings with this particular man often he is sure to know my favourite ploy and is thinking to himself: "Now he's on about the weather; another three minutes and he'll be getting to the point." Moreover, if you do not prepare for contact, you may fall into the trap of the celebrated dancing-lesson conversation: "Do you know Ibsen?" "No, how do you do that?"

Preparation for contact must be centred on two areas: the man you are talking to and the subject under discussion. It is obvious that not everyone responds to the same subject. Readiness to establish contact not infrequently depends on social status, level of education, age and even on where the other participant comes from.

Orientation towards the subject of the discussion means selecting the subject for contact talks so as to achieve a transition to the actual subject of the discussion after contact has been established without breaking this contact. If I wish to discuss a technical matter and start my discussion with a sports enthusiast by mentioning the result of the latest football match, it will be difficult to bring his attention back to the real matter at issue. A remark such as: "I think it's time for us to get down to business now" or "We could really spend hours talking about this but today we have to discuss something completely different" would disrupt the contact. Then the very thing we wished to achieve, bringing the other person in tune with the subject for discussion, has to be built up all over again.

The subject of contact talks should therefore bear some inner relationship – even if it is a tenuous one – to the subject of the ensuing discussion. If as host I have decided on a suitable subject, I must then consider at what point and under what conditions the transition should be made to the actual subject of the discussion. This transition must occur spontaneously.

To digress for a moment, it not only disrupts contact but is downright impolite if, after greeting his guest, the host continues to busy himself with other matters. "I hope you don't mind, but I must sign this letter." "I'm afraid I must just call someone on the 'phone." "If I may leave you on your own for two minutes, I'll be back directly." Then, after these important tasks have been attended to, there comes the relaxed leaning back in the armchair and the remark: "Well now, what can I do for you?" This is an unquestionable demonstration of priorities on the part of the host, indicating that the guest is regarded as considerably less important than the host's own preoccupations. As I have already said, from the first moment of contact between the two participants in a discussion, there can be nothing more important for these two people than the discussion itself and the people involved in it.

No "documents" are necessary for the contact phase. I once had a business associate who began his discussions by reading me an extract from a newspaper. "Wonderful that you came along this morning. I just happened to have read here . . ." He reaches towards the filing cabinet, rustles about among some newspapers. Finally he produces the financial section of a daily newspaper, leafs backwards and forwards, runs up and down the columns of print until he finds what he is looking for: "Here it says that the Minister made the following statement at the Annual General Meeting of the Ironmongers' Trade Association. . . ." (A lengthy verbatim quotation now follows. . . .). . "What do you think of that?" Searching for the newspaper, the word-for-word quotation, has the effect of inhibiting contact, and becomes tiresome. Basically there are no objections to using a topical reference to establish contact, but what is the point of the newspaper? What is the use of the exact quotation? Wouldn't it be less forced and more natural to express his in own words what it was that he found interesting in the article?

Fidgeting with objects also tends to inhibit contact. There are certain types of people who, hardly have they sat down to talk, pick up some object – a pencil, a ball-point pen, a matchbox or whatever is within easy reach. This behaviour is usually quite subconscious. If one mentions it to them they become extremely embarrassed and insist they did not realise that they had anything in their hand.

What does this fidgeting express? It is an indication of insecurity and nervousness. It is the expression of a subconscious desire to take a firm grip on something. They want to be in control of the situation and project an image of complete confidence, but their hands betray what is going on inside.

It is interesting to observe the behaviour of such people during the course of a discussion. As soon as they have recovered their confidence they suddenly and demonstratively put aside the object they are playing with, only to pick it up again when the discussion takes a difficult turn. How easy it is for one party in a discussion to recognise the weaknesses of the other! If you are one of those who like to "play", make sure at the beginning of the conversation that there are no objects within easy reach for you to fidget with.

It was stated earlier that the host is responsible for establishing contact. The guest for his part must give his host the chance of so doing. If the host does not exercise this "right", it is permissible for the guest to exert himself correspondingly. Silence or a generally phrased question on the part of the host may be regarded by the guest as an invitation to start the conversation and thereby establish contact.

If the host rejects the idea of contact from the very start, for instance with the words: "Please sit down. Let us get right down to business . . ." or asks questions such as: "Well, what's on your mind?" this must be regarded as an invitation to come to the main point of the discussion immediately. Should the guest at this point attempt frantically to introduce a contact phase, he could hardly be surprised to receive a more or less polite snub from his host, resulting in a real breakdown of contact. The fact that one of the participants may exclude a contact phase at the start of the conversation does not mean that the rest of the discussion must be conducted without personal contact. But it is considerably more difficult if contact is only established gradually during the course of the main discussion.

3 The honest, open gaze

Much can be done to establish contact even before a single word has been uttered. The total impression one gives can express an attitude of readiness or reluctance towards contact. The gaze, the facial expression, the posture and gestures can do more than any words to express this attitude.

The simplest but most effective means of establishing contact is with the eyes. I have to look at a person with whom I am trying to establish contact, or a person to whom I wish to express my readiness to do so. To look at someone does not mean to stare at them or fix them with a piercing gaze. It means that one should meet their gaze without any attitude of challenge. One reads so often in novels that lovers are only able to come to an understanding by gazing into each other's eyes. There is a great deal of truth in this. One can express joy, annoyance, astonishment, surprise and rejection through one's eyes without saying a single word. This fact is borne out by the expressions "cold eyes" and "friendly look" which are current in popular speech. There is, however, another saying in popular usage: "He can't even look me straight in the eye." Avoiding eye-to-eye contact is regarded as dishonest, furtive and deprecatory.

Not only the eyes, but also the expressions of the rest of one's features can contribute to establishing contact. A colleague of mine gives a very good example. As he says, if you enter a store where three saleswomen are unoccupied and waiting for customers, you instinctively approach the one who is looking at you in a friendly manner.

This principle is admirably expressed by the old Chinese proverb: "He who cannot smile should never open up shop." A friendly expression helps to establish contact. People who take part in a discussion without so much as moving a muscle of the face or allowing themselves to crack a smile, are in the long-run depressing. "Poker faced" or "dead pan" is how we describe them.

Even the way in which I physically approach the other person can encourage or inhibit contact. By taking a few steps towards my visitor to greet him, I help to establish contact. If on the other hand I stand behind my desk, remaining rather aloof and waiting for him to come to me, my attitude seems to be one of rejection. Gestures serve to strengthen contact. The simple invitation: "Please take a seat" has a quite different effect on the guest if accompanied by a suitable gesture of the hand, or by drawing back a chair for him to sit on. Likewise a relaxed and composed posture expresses readiness to enter into contact; someone who sits with his arms tightly folded gives the impression of being hard to approach.

4 Even in contact talks, certain subjects are taboo

Attention has already been drawn to the importance of choosing the correct subject for contact talks. Certain subjects should be avoided at all costs. Then there is a group which might be suitable, depending largely on who one is talking to. Finally there are a number of subjects which may be regarded as suitable for discussion in any situation.

As a general principle one ought not to broach subjects which might produce an emotional reaction in the other person. As already indicated, conversational taboos include politics, particularly party politics, religious and ideological beliefs, and illnesses. In saying that these subjects are unsuitable for establishing contact, I mean that I, as the person wishing to create the contact, should not of my own accord introduce them into a discussion. If a political discussion is to give the impression of honesty, it demands the complete personal involvement of those taking part. Particularly in this kind of discussion, any evasiveness or "toadying" is immediately recognised as dishonesty. The possibilities for making a smooth transition, without breaking contact, from a discussion on political topics of the day to the actual subject of the talks, are very slight indeed.

Economic questions and matters of regional policy are not necessarily regarded as political. If I wish to sell construction machinery, a discussion about current economic policy in the field of motorway construction can serve as a suitable entrée into the main discussion. If I wish to discuss the sale of a piece of land with those present, a development plan recently shelved by the local authority can be a useful point of reference from which to start the main talks. The important thing in such semi-political discussions is to concentrate exclusively on facts. An opinion should only be volunteered if the other person asks for it.

I do not think any further comments on religious and ideological beliefs are necessary.

For many people, illness seems to be an inexhaustible topic of conversation. No other subject admits of so many variations, ranging from the initial causes, symptoms and type of treatment to comparisons with other persons stricken by the same or a different disease. The innumerable aspects of this subject mean that there is a very real danger of the contact discussion developing into a full-scale debate.

There is another category of subjects which, although suitable for establishing contact, must be handled very carefully and tactfully. These are subjects in the "human–social" sphere, which are often recommended as suitable, but I have my doubts. Whether and to what extent I can touch on private matters in contact talks depends on a great number of things. First of all, considerable regional differences in attitude occur. If one asks a man from some parts of the country about his private life, his family, hobbies or similar topics during a business discussion, his reaction will be one of restraint. But in other parts people are more open and expect the personal side of their lives to be discussed. If I do not know the man in question and his attitude towards such subjects, I should try to avoid them. Even if I knew a lot about him I should only mention private matters if I am certain that by so doing I will get a positive reaction. An enquiry about a boy's performance at school can be extremely effective in establishing contact if the father is very proud of his son's achievements. If on the other hand he is indifferent or worse still, embarrassed to discuss his son's performance, this will have an adverse effect on his readiness to engage in contact.

A well-meaning enquiry about holidays can provoke very different types of reaction, according to how satisfactory or otherwise the holiday has been. If the man concerned has returned sunburnt, relaxed and contented, and if there were no unpleasant surprises awaiting him at work, he may react positively to this enquiry. If on the other hand he has just returned from spending two whole weeks in the pouring rain with his five children at the bleak seaside, and if on his return to work he had to deal with many awkward problems, the mere mention of the word holiday is likely to provoke an adverse reaction.

Another delicate subject which is often raised with the best of intentions when trying to establish contact is motor cars. Almost all men like talking about cars, especially if they own one. Consider the following fact: market research has established that only a small percentage of men wash themselves thoroughly from head to foot every day, yet the vast majority of men attach great value to having their car highly polished. Self-love is greatly surpassed by love for one's car. Talking about cars can be a very effective means of making contact, provided one can get the other person to talk about *his* car, *his* feats of motoring and *his* marathon drive home from holiday. If one succumbs to the temptation of comparing one's own achievements with his, ill-feeling is bound to result.

The same applies to hobbies. Almost everyone likes talking about his hobby, but not with just anyone or at any time of day.

If my hobby is church music or mediaeval literature, it can scarcely be regarded as a suitable introduction to a business discussion. Using one's hobby as a means of establishing contact can also appear importunate, tiresome and presumptuous to the other person. If one broaches the subject of hobbies it is necessary to show a degree of understanding, i.e. one ought to know a thing or two about the hobby to make one's interest credible. This credibility is achieved by showing an understanding of the rituals associated with the hobby, by using the correct expressions, and by being prepared to enter at least into a limited discussion of the subject.

Asking a sailing enthusiast when he was last sea-sick, or a hunter why he blasts away at the poor defenceless deer, is not simply a lack of understanding but is impertinent. If the other person is a football fan, then before embarking upon a football discussion I should at least take the trouble to find out which division his team plays in, its position in the league table and the result of the last match.

I once read in a newspaper that one could immediately establish contact with most people simply by mentioning the weather. Is talking about the weather really a suitable means of establishing contact? I think it is something of an embarrassment. After all, everybody is perfectly aware that it is raining at that very moment, or that the sun is shining, or that the weather has been too cool or rainy for the last few days. The weather is there for all to see and one can even listen to the forecasts. There is no reason why the weather should be discussed yet again.

Up to this point we have discussed only those subjects which should not be used for establishing contact or which should be treated with caution. Now we will consider subjects which are suitable for establishing and maintaining contact.

Once again we start from a small human weakness. Anyone invited to a discussion feels honoured. The first step towards making contact is the attempt to make the other person say something. The subject used for this purpose should bear some relationship to the subsequent topic of the discussion. For this purpose, a specific question is more honest than a general enquiry. The question: "Well, how are things with you?" expresses indifference and the person to whom it is directed realises that this same question is probably asked a dozen times a day. On the other hand, if I approach him on a specific matter, for instance "Yesterday I read such-and-such an article in the paper, did you see it? What did you think of it?" This gives the impression that I am not just concerned with our mutual problems but am also interested in him and his views.

Another effective way of establishing contact is to raise points of information, even if they are only tenuously related to the main topic of discussion, and to ask the other person to explain them. For a banker negotiating a credit problem with a customer, an item of information about the days' dealings on the stock market can provide a useful impulse for introductory talks.

The right atmosphere can also be created by mentioning any

D

personal or commercial successes which the other person has had; they could be concerned with his home life or with an institution with which he has connections.

5 "Heard this one . . . ?"

"The stock-exchange fulfills an economic function: without it, new jokes would take much longer to get round". Tucholsky came to this conclusion in 1931. In the old days the reply to the speculator's question: "What's the latest?" would invariably take the form of the latest stock exchange joke for a joke was part of the ritual of opening a discussion.

One cannot generalise about this way of starting today's business. Whether and to what extent humour may be used to initiate a discussion depends on the situation and on the relationship between the participants. Among friends and good acquaintances a "leg-pull" which to outsiders seems to be almost a verbal insult can be effective in creating a suitable atmosphere. A customer with whom I was on very close terms would frequently start off by saying something like: "You see, old boy, there is something in superstition after all. As I was leaving home this morning a black cat crossed my path. I said to myself that if there is any truth in superstition, something very unpleasant would happen to me today. And what happens? Half an hour later you're sitting with me in the office." A liberating burst of laughter follows: the atmosphere for the discussion has been created.

The humorous approach must be adapted to the personalities of those concerned. A sense of humour is not something which can be easily acquired. Any attempt to show oneself as a witty individual may produce the reverse effect.

It is better to start a discussion in a low emotional key rather than with a great show of exuberance, which it will be impossible to sustain when the technical details of the subject come to be discussed. It is all very well to crack jokes at a party, but restraint is recommended in business discussion.

6 "To my great reget . . ."

Recently I heard the following story:

Stanforth has some shares about which he has misgivings. "The Annual General Meeting takes place tomorrow from twelve to two o'clock," he says to his assistant. "Attend the meeting and let me know by telegram at two o'clock how things stand."

The assistant goes to the meeting. A telegram arrives at five minutes past twelve: "Sell immediately".

The assistant is praised when he returns from the meeting: "Thanks to you I was able to avoid considerable losses," says the boss. "But how were you able to send a telegram at twelve o'clock, before anybody else at the Exchange knew how things were going?"

"The chairman", explained the clerk, "opened the General Meeting with the words: 'Unfortunately . . .'. As soon as I heard that I knew everything."

A discussion must start and finish on a positive note. Contact can never be established on a negative basis. This applies both to what is discussed and how it is discussed. Imagine yourself in the following situation. You enter your boss's office. He asks you to take a seat and addresses you with the words: "My dear Robinson, unfortunately another letter has arrived this morning . . ."

Or you arrive for an appointment with a customer. He greets you with the words: "I am glad to see you, but unfortunately . . ."

Your telephone rings. It is your wife calling. "Sorry for ringing you at the office, but I'm afraid . . ."

What do you actually feel when you hear the word "unfortunately"? Inwardly, you immediately assume a defensive position, you become tense and inhibited. "Unfortunately" heralds something unpleasant. "Unfortunately" signifies bad news. Human language contains many words and phrases which provoke the same reaction: "Unfortunately", "To my great regret", "It is difficult for me to say this, but . . .", "I can imagine more pleasant things". Such remarks exert a negative influence on the atmosphere. Their significance is often emphasised by an appropriate tone of voice. Introductory phrases like these are delivered in a subdued and quiet voice, with declining emphasis. And refuge is often taken in any documents which are to hand. The speaker avoids looking the person straight in the face and leafs through his papers instead. In embarrassment, notes or symbols are jotted down in the margins of documents. The bearer of ill tidings takes short, apprehensive glances at the other person, as if to make sure he hasn't run away. The whole approach is insincere. The underlying intention is to give the impression that the speaker finds it difficult to impart bad news, perhaps even that what he is obliged to say is contrary to his own convictions. The encounter is made more difficult for both parties.

In fact, I have no regrets at all. I am not really sorry for anything I am about to say. The discussion which has to be conducted is the product of exact deliberations and the result of a decision which I have taken in the interests of my company. My client has asked me to visit him to discuss non-observance of deadlines in the latest deliveries. What is the purpose of starting off the discussion with the words: "Unfortunately, delays in delivery have repeatedly occurred in the past, and today I find myself in the unpleasant position of having to discuss this matter with you." I am aware that there have been delays in delivery. I knew it from the moment my customer asked for this discussion, and have accordingly made careful preparations for it. So if anybody is sorry that there have been delays, it is not me but my customer. My customer can expect deliveries to be carried out in accordance with the terms of the contract. Therefore he can open the discussion with a completely clear conscience, with a concrete statement such as: "I would like to talk to you about the delays in delivery which have occurred in the last few weeks."

Imparting unwelcome information is not a good way to create a working atmosphere. Imagine the following situation within your firm. You have summoned a number of colleagues in order to prepare for a decision relating to the organisation of the company. You start the discussion with the words:

"Gentlemen, we are gathered here today to discuss such-and-such a problem. A few minutes before you arrived the data-processing department gave me a summary comparing sales and profits in the first quarter of this year with last year. This shows that our sales and profits have declined considerably, which means that we must take decisive measures to counteract this unfavourable trend."

How will your colleagues react to this? Will they now be ready to participate with complete commitment in a discussion of the problems of organisation? Certainly not. They will be trying to digest the information you have just given them, to work out what consequences it could have for them and their jobs.

Every negative statement can be formulated in a positive way, thereby achieving a motivational effect. There is no element of dishonesty in this; it is merely a different approach. Negative statements are, generally speaking, related to the past. Discussions, however, are intended to move things forward. The past is only of significance in so far as it provides points of reference for the future. I can adopt the following attitude towards an employee who has been very lax in his duties: "My dear Finlay, I am profoundly disturbed about your declining efficiency over the past few months and I am obliged to inform you that things cannot go on like this." Alternatively, I can put it in a more positive manner. "Mr. Finlay, I have asked you to come and see me so that we might consider what steps can be taken to help you regain your previous standard of efficiency." In the first case, Finlay will immediately withdraw into his shell and everything you have to say to him will be coloured by the thought: "He's got it in for me." In the second case, specific activities of Finlay's are brought into question and he will certainly be prepared to co-operate with you in improving his standard of efficiency.

Summarising, it may be said that in establishing contact the aim of the preliminary phase is to prevent or reduce inhibitions, to induce an inner relaxation in the other person and to increase the readiness to co-operate on both sides. Even if the subsequent discussion results in disagreements, both parties concerned will at least depart with the feeling: "The person I have been dealing with is fair, polite and co-operative." The doors of communication have not been closed. I have conducted hundreds of experimental discussions in which the same subjects were discussed with and without a contact phase. And there is no doubt that having a contact phase results in far more productive and satisfactory talks.

CHAPTER XI

The subject of the discussion

When the bridge of contact is strong enough to support discussions, one should then proceed to the actual matter in hand. This transition is a relatively difficult part of the discussion. I have already indicated how an ostentatious conclusion of the contact phase followed by an obvious transition to the subject of the discussion can easily cause a breach in contact. Remarks such as "If we could now get to the point", "I think that now we should turn our attention to the actual subject of this discussion", "And this brings us to the business of the day' , are an unmistakable indication to all concerned that the conversation up to that point had nothing to do with the central discussion. If the other person was the one who made the effort to build up the contact, he feels slighted.

It can, however, be made evident, without breaking the contact, that the main part of the discussion has been reached. The transition to the central topic and the arrangement of the discussion must be achieved naturally, and not by using standard expressions.

1 What do we wish to discuss today?

At the beginning of the real discussion comes the clarification of the subject for discussion among those taking part. The initiative here is taken by the person who instigated the talks. This is not necessarily the host; the guest also has this right.

If the subject is a complex one, it should be divided into manageable sections. This is particularly recommended when it seems probable that the subject under discussion will call for a whole series of talks. The most important questions can then be settled first. Other issues can be discussed during the subsequent course of the talks without there being any fear of neglecting things which one or other of the participants may have on his mind.

Many discussions suffer from being overburdened by content. The attempt is made to discuss too many subjects simultaneously: the overall view is lost and the discussion ends inconclusively. When the preparations for talks are being carried out the various questions to be discussed should be arranged in the most useful order.

If the talks are taking place on the initiative of one particular participant, it is his duty to explain his reasons for requesting the discussion. This should make it clear that it is in both parties' interests to meet. It is, for example, not so much a question of discussing declining sales with my customer but rather of discussing our future business relationship.

If the subjects to be treated in the discussion are not clearly established, there will be a risk that the talks will develop into a series of monologues. Everyone is attempting to realise his own expectations, with the result that no one achieves complete fulfilment of his aims and each leaves with a feeling of dissatisfaction.

2 Do we have the same objective in mind?

The importance of the objectives has already been mentioned. A discussion can only be conducted with a degree of finality if those taking part direct their arguments towards a common objective or if one participant fully accepts the declared aims of the other. Occasionally someone is heard to say: "He doesn't need to know what I have in mind. He'll soon realise what I'm getting at." This attitude is as naïve as it is incorrect. Naïve because in so many cases the intention behind the talks can be deduced from the mere desire to hold the talks.

If there is a ring at the front door and a man or a woman is standing there with a large case full of samples, the housewife realises that they want to sell something, even if the visitor opens the conversation by referring to the fact that he is conducting a market research poll for a certain product. If a bank manager

calls on a company director who has not hitherto been a client of
the bank's, he knows that the bank manager has not come to sing
hymns with him, but that he wishes to recruit another customer.
If I as sales manager request talks with the purchasing manager of
a client company on the subject of our general business relationship, the purchasing manager knows, when he prepares for the
discussion, what my general intentions and aims will be. Has
turnover declined? Have payment deadlines been overlooked?
What other problems have there been between the two firms?
Attempts to conceal the real intentions or aims behind the talks
only wring a weary smile from the other person. On the other hand
I gain his confidence if I openly declare my intentions. So always
put your cards on the table!

Honesty about one's intentions has another advantage. If my
customer objectively considers that my aims cannot be realised,
time and energy will be saved if the aims in question are modified
from the start and made more realistic. The possibilities for
realising these aims may be limited by the scope of authority of
one of the persons concerned. Perhaps this will only become
evident after stating the problem. For example, I am offering my
services as supplier to a new company. My enquiries have revealed
that the purchasing manager is authorised to take decisions on
matters of purchase. But when I state my intentions the purchasing
manager may tell me that although he has authority over all
matters of purchasing, the acceptance of new suppliers is a matter
which must be decided at general management level. It would
therefore be pointless for me to submit offers to the purchasing
manager before a decision had been made at management level as
to whether my firm should be recruited as a supplier.

Likewise if as purchasing manager I wish to enter into discussions with my supplier's sales manager about shortening
delivery dates, and the sales manager explains at the outset that
this is technically impossible, there would be no point in presenting
further arguments with a view to changing the terms of the
contract.

The initiative for establishing the objective of a discussion as
well as the subject of the talks should be taken by the instigator

of the talks. If the various parties' objectives seem to be divergent, an order of precedence must be worked out for their respective aims. A client asks the credit manager of his bank for a discussion of their present business relationship. His intention is to obtain an extension of a special credit which will become due for payment in the next few days. The credit manager of the bank on the other hand wishes to use the opportunity to discuss the declining sales on the export market. In a case like this the priority of their respective aims should be mutually agreed upon by both parties before embarking upon a discussion of either subject.

3 Are we working from the same background information?

One reason for discussions taking an undesired course is frequently found in the discrepancy between the respective points of departure of the participants, particularly discrepancies in the information which each has at his disposal. What information should the participants have to conduct an objective discussion?

First a number of important preliminary questions should be clarified. Are we both working from the same commercial situations? If I wish to discuss the development of sales of occasional furniture with a purchasing manager, it should be clear from the start that we are both referring to the same set of sales statistics. Possibly one of us may possess a more up-to-date set of figures which could be of decisive importance for the ensuing discussion. Are our comparisons of turnover based on the same basic data? For example, I may be comparing sales in the first three months of this year with sales in the first three months of the previous year, while the other person may be relating this year's sales to the mean turnover in the previous year. On this basis he will of course arrive at a different result. Again, if national statistics are used for comparison purposes, we must make sure that both sides are drawing their information from the same sources. My colleague may be using data issued by a government department, while my statistics have been issued by a trade association. Considerable differences may occur which can throw a completely different light on the figures.

D*

Moreover, is he familiar with a certain exchange of correspondence which I would like to refer to in the discussion? Is he fully informed about conversations which have taken place between his colleagues and mine which will have significance in my arguments?

Are both sides using the same concepts? Specialists develop their own language. This often by-passes traditional usage. If I wish to discuss occasional furniture with the other person, then I ought to know whether the description "occasional furniture" means the same to him as it does to me. Some time ago I had a discussion with a pleasant young lady, who was the press representative of a large factory, about her company's products. In our conversation mobile stairs were repeatedly mentioned.

I imagined all manner of things. Mobile stairs? It became evident later in our conversation that the travelling stairs in question were what is more commonly known as an escalator. After this had become clear many points in our conversation took on a quite different aspect. Are we on the same wavelength where other matters are concerned? Do we share the same assessment of the current market situation? Do we have different ideas on the present state of competition? Do we start from different assumptions? Perhaps I view certain commercial developments primarily from a national perspective, while the other person sees things from a regional viewpoint. Clearing up such issues should not be deferred until an argument has arisen due to misunderstandings.

4 Do I have the necessary authority to deal with the other people's requirements?

The point has been made repeatedly that in a business discussion the function, authority, position or responsibilities of the participants are very significant. Board members would discuss a subject in a different way from the heads of departments. If the question is whether commercial relationships should be taken up with another firm, members of the board will discuss whether the new connection would be useful to general company policy. They will not usually talk about prices, conditions of delivery, or the technical problems involved. These matters would be the concern of lower levels in the administration. Nor is it the duty of a board member to be thoroughly acquainted with the details of such problems. He has at his disposal departmental heads who submit reports on these matters.

At the departmental head level, on the other hand, the decisions of the board and their consequences for various departments should be discussed. However, it would not be their concern to discuss detailed questions relating to daily work processes. Questions such as how many printed forms to use, how many copies of documents should be submitted and to whom and so on are matters for their subordinates. Every level in the company has its specific set of problems to attend to.

Since the organisation and allocation of duties varies widely from company to company (determined partly by the size of the company) it is important for the person having discussions to establish at the outset his opposite number's authority and responsibilities, so that the scope of the discussion can be tailored accordingly. There is nothing more wearying and depressing than, on reaching the decisive point in a discussion to be told: "I'm afraid I can't say anything definite on this; it is a matter for our management committee" (or "In our company this is not a matter for the sales department but for central administration").

If the participants in a discussion are not sufficiently clear about each other's functions and authority, the inevitable result will be time-wasting and ultimately, pointless manoeuvring. What can I tell the other person? How far can I show my hand? Am I perhaps creating difficulties for future talks by discussing these questions with him rather than with the person who really has the authority to deal with them?

Since this question consciously or unconsciously overshadows almost every discussion in which the participants and their functions are unknown to each other, the answer should be obtained at the start. Agreement about the subjects to be discussed and about the objective of the talks provides a good opportunity to establish each other's areas of responsibility. This initiative for clarifying the question of competence should be taken by the person who suggested having the discussion in the first place. The talks can then be begun something like this: "I asked to have this discussion with you so that we can determine the delivery dates relevant to our contract." In this way it is clear that I am authorised to establish delivery dates. It is also evident that my authority is limited to the contract in question. My introductory sentence further implies that negotiations regarding deviations from the terms of the contract do not come within the scope of my authority.

5 How shall we proceed?

In most cases business discussions do not take place in isolation, but are enmeshed in a whole web of relationships between the different departments concerned. Discussions have already taken place on the particular subject, and probably will take place again in the future. The talks which I have with one person can provide a point of departure for further discussions between other executives in the other company and in my own.

A building contractor wishes to purchase a new photocopying machine. This decision sparks off a series of discussions. First of all the sales manager of the supplying firm pays a courtesy visit to the contractor, describing the advantages of dealing with his firm. He offers references and visits to satisfied users. After this introductory talk there follows a series of discussions on various levels. The specialists of the supplying company consult with the contractor's drawing office, with their architect and with the employees who will later be operating the machine. Visits are made to firms where this machine is already in operation. Invitations are issued for demonstrations or to visit the next trade fair or exhibition. Then come discussions about servicing, cost of materials and finally delivery and installation. After this a firm and final quotation is issued and, perhaps after further negotiations, the sales contract is signed. While these complex, interrelated discussions, which were sparked off by one single approach, are going on it is the task of the principle department concerned to maintain an overall view and to direct the series of negotiations towards completion.

It is the duty of this administrative department at the start of the negotiations to arrange the anticipated discussions systematically and chronologically. To this end each participant in the talks should work out a list of questions which need to be discussed and negotiated. The first round of talks should then be devoted to establishing which of the people involved should be brought into contact with each other for discussions. In addition it should be established in what order and when certain discussions should be concluded. All those participating in the subsequent talks must be informed about what is being discussed and when. The administrative deparment must ensure that the schedule is adhered to and should from time to time keep the various participants informed about intermediate results. If these intermediate results raise new problems, the departments concerned should co-operate in modifying the subject and time schedules.

Only exact advance planning of subjects and dates makes it possible to avoid the far too common practice of discussing the same matter, under different headings, at widely differing administrative levels, without any liaison between the various negotiators. It is even possible that interim decisions are made at different levels which contradict each other and which have undesirable consequences for both sides.

An essential factor in planning such a series of talks is discipline among those concerned. Unnecessary prolongation of detailed negotiations endangers the total project by creating a time shortage. An integral part of establishing the discussions must therefore be an agreement on procedure, i.e. the actual course of the negotiations, irrespective of who controls them.

6 How much time do we have available?

The secretary who enters her boss's office with the message that he is required to attend a board meeting to relcase him from a seemingly interminable discussion is now a standard in the traditional repertoire of office jokes. As is usually the case, the joke has a grain of truth in it. The participants entered a discussion with conflicting ideas about the time limit involved. While the host had only anticipated a short conversation, the guest intended to use the opportunity for exhaustive negotiations. This constantly recurring situation causes annoyance and dissatisfaction on both sides. An agreement on the length of the discussion is necessary to create a healthy working atmosphere.

The relationship between the length of the discussion and the capacity for concentration has already been mentioned. However, there is an additional point. The participants must be able to incorporate the time taken up by the discussion into their respective work schedules. It may be assumed that nowadays everyone in business has his own fairly full work schedule. Any serious distortion of this schedule endangers subsequent arrangements and possibly the entire work schedule. With this in mind it seems obvious that an agreement as to the subject and the aim of the discussions should be accompanied by an agreement as to their length.

The length of the discussions helps to determine which subjects are to be treated and the *order* in which they should be approached. Only by careful planning can one avoid the situation where there is no time left to discuss certain topics. A common error is to save the most important items on the agenda for the end of the discussions. But time becomes scarce at the end. The result is that the most important matters receive only superficial attention.

The duration of a discussion should be agreed when making the appointment because it is fairer to tell one's opposite number when fixing the time and place: "I would be glad to place myself at your disposal tomorrow afternoon from 3 to 4 p.m.", than for him to arrive at 3 p.m., start the discussion, and then be informed shortly before 4 p.m.: "I'm afraid that is all I have time for, I am expecting another visitor at 4."

On the other hand it is the duty of both participants in a discussion to keep to the arranged times. A visitor who consents to a time limit of one hour for a discussion, thinking: "Well, wait until I'm there, we'll soon see whether an hour will be sufficient", violates the conventions of a negotiation just as much as the man who uses his secretary to bring a discussion to an arbitrary conclusion.

PART THREE

The discussion

CHAPTER XII

Modern forms of discussion

It has recently become fashionable to "discuss" things. Students interrupt lectures with demands for a discussion. Political speeches are brought to an abrupt conclusion with chants of "Discussion, discussion". In schools there are demands for discussions with the teachers. Does all this represent a new discovery or is it just a revival of something long forgotten?

I do not wish to remind you of the numerous images which we associate with the concept "discussion". We do not find discussion easy. It is an old form of verbal intercourse which went out of fashion. Discussion is perhaps the oldest form of interpersonal relationship. Not command and obedience, but discussion has for more than two thousand years been the basis of human relationships. It was so in ancient Greece as well as in Rome and under the joint administration system of the Hanseatic trading cities of North Germany.

The army was the first organisation to introduce absolute authority in all its variations, to put an end to discussion and to replace it with a command/obedience relationship. "Theirs not to reason why, theirs but to do and die", is the slogan of soldiers of the king and it expresses the essential relationship between authority and submission.

The right to demand and enforce obedience by virtue of a superior position transferred itself from the army to the State, from the State to the economy, but also from the State to the family and other interpersonal structures. Daily experience provides us with hundreds of examples. Authority and discussion are mutually exclusive. When authority diminishes, a way to have discussions is sought. But discussion is not simply a matter of good intentions. The ability to discuss things is something which must be learned.

The revival of the principle of discussion took place during the French Revolution. Responsible citizens wanted to determine the course of their own fate. The hierarchy of official authority had been abolished by the revolution. Belief in reason replaced the belief in the divine right of Kings. And whenever reasonable people discuss together, the majority, it is thought, represents the voice of reason. On the basis of this premise, the first few years of the French Revolution were characterised by the excellent quality of public discussion. Majorities were formed by the power of reason. Thus to the present day, France is regarded as the homeland of discussion. Anyone who has had the opportunity to take part in a discussion with Frenchmen will be able to confirm that this belief is justified.

In countries where there has been no radical solution such as the French Revolution, but where instead a modern state has developed from concessions made by an authoritarian system, in other words in the constitutional monarchies such as England, something else has developed: the debate. The debate is designed to allow the petitioner the opportunity of forcing authority to grant him rights and concessions. The purpose and consequence of a discussion and a debate are therefore fundamentally different.

1 Let's leave debating to Parliament

The term debate derives from the French work "battre", to beat. The participants in a debate as it were beat each other with their preconceived opinions. The purpose of a debate is not to convince one's opponent, but to defeat him. Popular speech shows a particular sensitivity towards this distinction. There is a quite conscious distinction between a parliamentary debate and a committee discussion. We speak of internal party discussions, but of debates at party conferences. Here we can see most clearly where the boundaries are drawn.

We enter into parliamentary debates when the discussions within the party or between the various party factions have been concluded. The speakers in the debate only present the arguments which have contributed to forming internal party policy. There is little possibility of a change of attitude, except for concessions made on points of detail in the more intimate "committee stages" of passing new legislation. The compulsion exercised by political parties is directly related to full-scale parliamentary debating procedures.

A good friend of mine, a high government official, once said to me: "It does not matter whether I am right or not, but that I uphold the law." It would be difficult to summarise more concisely the meaning of the term debate. Whenever demonstrators disturb public meetings with the call for discussion, whenever the academic teaching routine in the universities is disrupted by demand for discussion, there is in fact no desire or readiness for discussion, but rather the wish to enter into debate.

Unfortunately the parliamentary model exerts an influence on interpersonal relationships. Many discussions suffer from the fact that one or more of the participants is simply no longer concerned with *talking with the other person*. What he is trying to do is to force his opinion, his attitude to the problem, his conclusions, on to the other person. This method has dire results. You cannot hear if you have no wish to listen. You do not wish to listen if you have entered into a discussion with preconceived opinions and if you are not prepared to make the slightest concession to the other person. He must accept your view of the matter totally and completely. He must recognize your argument as the only correct interpretation of the facts. Whatever he himself has to say only gets in the way and prolongs the discussion unnecessarily.

2 A talk between friends is also a discussion

As already mentioned, the origin of the discussion is quite different from that of the debate. The basic assumption behind the discussion is that there are various opinions on a certain subject on which consultation is desirable. In contrast to the debate, the participant in a discussion is not intent upon winning through with his argument at all costs. By comparing his opinion with other opinions on the subject he wants to find the best, or shall we say most reasonable, solution.

The word "discussion" derives from the Latin word "discutere", to shake thoroughly. A discussion can be compared to the mixing of a cocktail. Various opinions are put together in a mixer. They are shaken up thoroughly and the result is a single drink which is a combination of all the different constituents. It is often said contemptuously that discussion results in compromise, and a compromise is always the weakest solution. This view represents a much too simple relationship between cause and effect. The participants in a discussion should represent their own opinions, fight for their own views, but they must nevertheless also be prepared to make concessions and to be receptive to other points of view. A discussion should be a form of co-operation from the outset. Its outcome will normally be not a victory for one party, but a completely new "mix", distinct from the ingredients contributed to it.

Viewed in this light, discussion with all its various techniques should be the essence of every kind of interpersonal communication. Duden translates the word "discussion" as "exchange of opinions", the accent being on the idea of exchange.

If one subscribes to the general assertion that the basis of modern economics is co-operation (in which competition is only a special form of co-operation), then it follows that the essence of this co-operation is discussion between those willing to co-operate and we must allow ourselves to be governed much more closely by the basic principles of discussion in our interpersonal relationships, be this in the economic or the social sphere.

Now we shall turn our attention to the three basic techniques which constitute discussion: the question, the statement and the summary.

CHAPTER XIII

The art of asking questions

The question and not the statement is the most important aid to controlling or even beginning a discussion. The questioner has the initiative, rather than the person who is merely stating facts. The question makes it easier to state facts, because it stimulates a flow of information from the other person and this forms the basis of subsequent statements.

A question can rebuff the person to whom it is directed. It can be offensive and retard the discussion. A question should be designed to help and not to hinder the other person in speaking. For this reason, it is important that a question should be presented in the correct form.

1 "You must admit I'm right. . . ."

When I visit friends who regard themselves as connoisseurs of tea, I have a drink placed before me which these good people consider to be tea. This is accompanied by the comment: "As a connoisseur of tea, you must admit that this is an exceptionally good brand." What am I to do? If I answer, "Yes, I must say, this is exceptionally good tea", I am dishonest. If I say, ' 'It's dishwater!' this is extremely rude and uncalled for. After lengthy consideration I have decided that, whenever this situation occurs, to answer: "I have never tasted tea like this before."

Far more frequently than we realise, we use the type of question which, as just illustrated, presents the other person with two alternatives: politeness or honesty. This is the suggestive question: "You must admit I'm right . . ."; "In this case any sensible person would say . . . or do you have a different opinion?"; "I'm sure that I have brought a series of important new facts to your attention, haven't I?" Have you ever kept a check on yourself to see how often you use expressions like these?

What do I expect from the man I am talking to? Do I really hope for a sincere and honest answer? Generally speaking, no. I am looking for approbation. I want to have the correctness of my thoughts, conclusions and assertions confirmed by him.

For this reason the suggestive question is used in situations in which the other person has no alternative, whether this be due to a relationship of dependency, politeness or tactfulness, than to give the answer that you really want to hear. As a senior executive, a parent or teacher, one ought to consider how often one may be conditioning the responses of another person towards dishonesty by using suggestive questions. These should never arise in a well-conducted discussion.

Years ago it was widely believed in the sales training world that the concluding phase of the discussion, which ought to terminate in an actual sale, should be gradually induced by the use of suggestive questions of an increasingly restricting nature, until the sale was effected. On the basis of personal experience I should like to issue a warning about this technique. The aim in selling is to convince another person, not to take him by surprise. Therefore he must be allowed complete freedom to make his own independent decisions right up to the very end of the talk. It is impossible to convince someone by means of suggestive questions.

2 Can honesty be tested by catch questions?

Recently I was told about an executive who, when the office was shut, would ask his secretary under some pretext or other to take files or other documents from the desks or filing cabinets of his staff and would inspect them for mistakes. If he found some small error, for instance that certain correspondence had not yet been settled, or that stamps or signatures were missing, the following morning he would summon the person in question and would ask quite casually during a conversation on a completely different subject: "Are your files all in correct order. Is there anything overdue or are there any difficulties?" If the person answered – either in good faith or because he had intended to settle the small matter that very day – that everything among his papers was in order, there would follow a moral dressing-down, including such expressions as "lies" and "dishonesty" and "unworthy".

When questioned about this practice, and asked why he did not come straight out with his questions, the executive answered that now and again it was necessary for him to test the honesty of his staff. Catch questions are often used as a means of testing honesty. But can honesty be tested by means of such questions? I don't think so. I am inclined to think that anyone adopting this technique lives in fear of being swindled.

Apart from a few pathological liars, no one really likes to be dishonest. People usually only cheat and lie when they have no alternative. The clerk who feels that he is being "crowded" by his superior almost to the point of verbal insult, attempts to withdraw from this situation. The client who thinks that an honest answer on his part will give rise to commercial difficulties will give an evasive answer. Men who have confidence in each other do not need to resort to such tricks. A professional swindler will never be caught out by catch questions. It is only the small-time people who fall for them.

Catch questions and suggestive questions have no place in a well-conducted discussion.

3 "When may I come?" – "When did you have in mind"?

Another common failing in discussions is not to answer a question directly, but to reply with another question. Marital arguments, I am told, consist exclusively of a series of mutual questions.

Answering a question with another question has an alienating effect. It often means that one wishes to make it clear to the other person that he is unable to present his questions so that they can be answered unambiguously. Or it can mean that one is trying to avoid answering a specific question and to weaken its effect or change the subject by asking a question of one's own.

For example, if the husband asks his wife, when she returns home late after a shopping spree: "Where have you been so long?" and if she answers: "Are you afraid I've spent too much?", this is obviously an attempt to manoeuvre the conversation in a different direction.

It is a particularly bad conversational habit to answer a question with another question. Every question should be approached in a positive way. If the initial question is too vaguely formulated, then the question must be made more precise so that one can give a satisfactory answer; asking another question to this end can be justified. But in most cases responding with a counter question expresses an attitude of aggression and even rejection.

4 Chain questions are an encouragement to "help oneself"

"I've been looking forward to seeing you very much; please tell me what your current price limits are, what discounts you grant for purchases of ten, twenty and a hundred tons, what your earliest delivery dates are, what method of dispatch you employ, whether you deliver ex-works or free to the purchaser, whether transport insurance is to be covered by you or us, how the invoices are to be made out, i.e. whether you draw up part-payment invoices or whether we pay you in instalments and then receive a final invoice from you?"

What are the consequences of such a barrage of questions? The person to whom they are directed can react in three different ways. He can concentrate on the first question and prepare his answer accordingly. In this case all the subsequent questions simply pass him by without lodging in his consciousness. He can turn his attention exclusively to answering the last in the series of questions, because he has been waiting for the questioner to reach the end of his catalogue of inquiry. The last question will have remained in his mind. He will seize upon it in order to make some response. The third possibility is that he will select from the plethora of questions the one which suits him best, i.e. the one which is the easiest to answer and presents the least number of difficulties. If, however, he should want to answer the chain of questions exhaustively, he will have to ask the other person again and again to repeat his questions. This will prove very annoying to both parties.

A distinction must be drawn between chain questions and the arrangement of a complex subject into manageable sections for discussion. We shall be returning to this technique shortly.

5 Rhetorical questions sound theatrical

"And finally I ask myself the question; how is this going to come about? And now I should like to tell you the conclusion I arrived at." Although rhetorical questions are certainly useful for enlivening speeches and lectures, by giving the listener the impression that he is being addressed in person, they are out of place in discussions. In a discussion, a person is addressed directly. He expects that if questions are asked, he as a participant in the discussion must answer them. He does not expect to hear the answer from the person asking the question. Thus rhetorical questions inevitably sound artificial and theatrical in the intimacy of a discussion. The same idea would be much simpler and more effective put as follows: "I am here to tell you my ideas about our future collaboration."

There is an even more dramatic effect if the rhetorical question is coupled with a suggestive question. For instance: "Again and again I have asked myself how can I solve this problem. And if you've had any experience of business you have to admit that business ethics are no longer the same as they were twenty years ago." It is completely without interest what questions the participant in a discussion has been asking himself. The other party is only interested in the result.

CHAPTER XIV

Questions can be open and closed

So far we have discussed what questions should not be used in discussions. Let us now turn our attention to questions which can be used. The question with which I can begin, enliven, continue and conclude the discussion, is the objective, unambiguous question in various degrees of concentration. When asking the question, honesty and directness are always preferable to the evasive approach.

1 "Please answer yes or no"

There was once a magistrate who had insisted to an accused person in court that it was possible to answer any question by saying "Yes" or "No". When the accused asked whether he might ask the judge a question, the magistrate, true to his principles, answered with a clear and simple "Yes". He then asked the judge: "My Lord, do you still beat your wife as violently as you used to?" The judge never again repeated his assertion.

Questions which one can answer simply with "yes" or "no" or with a correspondingly short and concise statement, are closed questions. "What was the rate of turnover last month?" "Has a reply been sent to the complaint from Blackdown and Co.?" "What is the current rate of illness?" "When does Mr. Briggs return from holiday?" These are closed questions. The purpose is to supply the questioner with specific items of information. A conversation is brought to an end when an answer has been supplied to a closed question. If a series of closed questions are asked one after the other, the resulting impression is of interrogation. The latitude for the questioned person to develop his own thoughts and ideas has been restricted from the start.

No discussion can be conducted exclusively on the basis of closed questions. Nevertheless, there will hardly ever be a discussion in which closed questions are not used to establish certain basic facts. If the delivery period for certain goods plays a part in a decision as to whether or not to purchase goods from a prospective supplier, it is necessary at some point to ask a specific question about deliveries. An employee outlining a business matter to his superior must be prepared to answer specific questions. However, in any discussion great care must be taken to ensure that the necessity for extracting information does not result in a series of closed questions, where finally, instead of participants in a discussion, there is only the magistrate facing the accused person. After every closed question one should endeavour to re-open the discussion by, for instance, seeking further explanations of the answer or perhaps by giving the questioned person an opportunity to ask his own questions.

2 "What were your holidays like?"

The above is an open question. Open questions admit of a multitude of answers. "What were your holidays like?" "How are things at home"? "What's new?" Or the stereotype question which seems to follow almost every business trip: "Well, what was it like in Chicago?" The open question presented in this extreme form has certain advantages, but they are accompanied by pitfalls.

The advantage of the very open question, for the person opening the conversation, is that the other person can be unobtrusively given the lead. He is given freedom to introduce any subject into the discussion which comes within the scope of the open question. This improves the general atmosphere, allows the questioned person to relax and finally also makes it possible for the questioner to find out what significance the other man attributes to various matters. In the meantime he himself has a chance to recharge his mental batteries.

The possible disadvantages of open questions are that the questioned person may answer very hesitantly or evasively and that the answer may take a completely different turn from that anticipated. The husband returning from a business trip to Paris is asked by his wife: "Well, how was Paris?" The husband's answer: "Oh, quite strenuous." The wife's reaction: "You've just spent a week in Paris, and all you can say is that it was quite strenuous." The husband's reaction here was not an attempt to evade an honest answer. It was simply not clear to him what his wife wanted to know. Did she want to know what he had seen or which acquaintances he had met, where his accommodation was, or how he had spent his evenings? Refuge is taken in generalities to avoid being tied down to specific answers.

A very openly formulated question can leave the person in doubt about the sort of answer which is expected. This uncertainty can result in tension if the questioner, instead of making his question more specific, addresses initially good humoured but gradually more irate requests to the other person to give a specific answer. The other person, he thinks, must be concealing something. Or perhaps something has gone awry. This sort of situation does not help to create a co-operative atmosphere.

3 "I would suggest to start with that we discuss the first major point . . ."

An open question is certainly appropriate for the beginning of a discussion. However, one should give some consideration, when preparing for the discussion, to how open questions, used at the outset to define the discussion, may be subsequently broken down into manageable topics for discussion. This needs to be done in such a way that the other party is given an overall view of the problem and can organise his thoughts accordingly.

The open question does not in fact need to be formulated as a question: it can also be expressed in the form of a statement. Instead of asking my colleague Tomlinson who has just returned from a business trip to Chicago: "Well, my dear Tomlinson, how were things in Chicago?" I can start the conversation: "Mr. Tomlinson, I would like to talk to you about your business trip to Chicago; what interests me particularly is which customers you visited, whether these customers were satisfied with the service provided by our company, and what new contacts you managed to establish. Let's start with the customers you visited there." I have achieved two things by starting the conversation in this manner. I have indicated the range to be covered by the conversation and I have made it clear to the other person, by means of the individual questions, which in turn are formulated as open questions, what I would like to talk to him about. Within the individual questions he has sufficient latitude to develop his own thoughts and so take the initiative.

This technique can be used not only at the start of a conversation. Subsequently, when there is a difficult situation or when the discussion threatens to grind to a halt, multi-pronged open questions can provide a means of bypassing a bottleneck. Finally, the open question is useful if it becomes necessary to narrow down a conversation which has become too diffuse or to bring the discussion to a conclusion.

CHAPTER XV

Statements

Conversation is not, as has already been mentioned, borne along exclusively by questions, but also by the answers which are given to these questions. The form of the statement, the facts and ideas expressed in it exert a decisive influence on the atmosphere and progress of a discussion.

There are two basic forms of statement: the factual statement and the opinion. A clear distinction must as far as possible be maintained between fact and opinion in a discussion. However, the boundaries between these two types are somewhat fluid. Even when making a selection of the facts which have been presented, a great deal of opinion and personal involvement can come into play. On the other hand, many statements are formulated as opinions, although basically they are an expression of facts.

1 According to the latest figures published by the Government . . .

A particular form of statement is the factual statement in which sources are quoted. This statement is neutral in value. Even if the factual statement is supported by documentary evidence it is not unassailable. The source which is given can be placed in doubt. One can also dispute the right to substantiate one's personal statements by quoting an official source. However, the fact itself is beyond all doubt.

No discussion can be conducted exclusively on the basis of documented factual statements. The atmosphere of the court room is induced if the other party is asked to substantiate every statement he makes with documentary evidence. It should be remembered that every discussion requires the personal engagement of the individual participants.

2 "I stand by what I have said"

In discussions one so often hears: "That's what you say, but can you prove it?" This illustrates the distance between the documented factual statement and the assertion. An assertion is a statement of fact without any proof. Generally speaking, the assertion should also include a factual statement. One asserts that one has done or not done some particular thing. It is maintained that one has read or seen something of a particular nature. The assertion is made that a certain event occurred in such and such a way. The reaction to an assertion can be a counter-assertion or a hypothetical supposition. If an assertion is met by a counter-assertion, the discussion is in grave danger. Assertions and counter-assertions tend to result in an argument. If this is to be avoided, try to reach alternative solutions by means of hypothetical suppositions. Finally, assertions and counter-assertions can be substantiated or put in doubt by means of a documented factual statement.

An assertion is not necessarily a factual statement; it can also be an expression of opinion. "I maintain that anybody who says he has never had any trouble with his XYZ car is not telling the truth." In this case the experiences of the person speaking have resulted in his holding a definite opinion which he already regards as having the value of fact. Such opinions, disguised as facts, threaten to turn discussions into arguments.

3 Isn't everybody corruptible in the last analysis?

A distinction must be made between the assertion presented in the form of a seriously intended factual statement and the so-called provocative assertion. The provocative assertion is not meant to be a factual statement in the true sense of the term, but is intended either by its form or by its content to provoke the other person into expressing a contradictory opinion, or at the very least into making a factual statement of his own. The provocative assertion can be formulated both as a statement and as a question. There is a nice little story attributed to a 19th century banker. When he was once asked whether it was correct that his annual income was more than £1m., he denied this. Then a provocative assertion that his earnings were greater was disguised in the form of another question: "And what would you do if you did make £1m. a year?" The banker immediately detected the intention behind this question and replied: "I would cut down on expenses."

The provocative assertion is a very risky form of statement and conversational technique. It can of course be very witty and stimulate a witty riposte. However, it demands a high degree of sensitivity and appreciation on the part of the other person. Very few people understand provocative assertions of this nature and react to them in a suitable manner. Most people regard a provocative assertion as a real assertion and, according to their temperament, react either with annoyance or indignation.

4 "Let us just assume . . ."

The hypothesis is a conversational aid which, as already mentioned, is frequently used to deal with assertions. It can also be used as an independent statement. Hypotheses are employed when it is impossible to make definite factual statements. Let us assume that I am a salesman visiting a client, and that during my visit it is asserted that the machine which we have delivered has shown certain defects; I will not be in a position to assume any particular attitude about these technical problems and the resulting complaints. Nevertheless, it is expected that I, as the seller of the machine, will express some reaction. The most that I am able to say in such a situation is: "Assuming that your statements are correct, of course we would be prepared to grant a reduction in price corresponding to the reduced performance of the machine."

The second possibility, as already mentioned, is to neutralise assertions and counter-assertions by means of hypothetical solutions. In such a situation one can proceed by suggesting to the other person: "Since we are unable to clear up the situation for the moment, I suggest that first of all we discuss the consequences arising from your assertion, and that we then discuss the implications if my assertion proves to be correct." In a case like this the hypothesis is used primarily as a form of reaction. However, the hypothesis can also be used as a factual statement, as in the following example: "Admittedly we do not yet have the results of the analysis, but on the basis of intermediate results up to this point I think we can assume that . . ."

The hypothesis has one great danger. It has a tendency to branch off into irrelevant mental exercises. There is always a large element of uncertainty when you start with an hypothesis. The greater the uncertainty, the more numerous the options which can be taken as the starting-point for hypotheses. In this way one can arrive at the most farcical conclusions. If a hypothesis is to be employed at all, it must be based on a small and realistic number of possibilities.

5 "Probably this is another case of . . ."

The concept of the "assumption" is hard to define. It can be used in much the same way as an hypothesis, but it can also be used to impute certain things to a person. We have left the factual sphere and have entered the realm of expressed opinions.

If I impute something to someone or if in a particular situation I assume a certain pattern of behaviour or a certain course of events, then I am placing what is commonly known as experience in a special relationship to fact. An order has not been delivered punctually. That is a fact. My experience tells me that in the majority of such cases the cause lies with the carelessness of the dispatch department. Therefore I express the opinion: "If it was not sent off punctually, that probably means the dispatch department has slipped up again." It will only be possible to establish whether this is correct by examining the facts.

This kind of statement of opinion is dangerous. In most conversations an assumption signifies a reversal of the burden of proof. In the case of a customer, who is complaining about delays in delivery and who assumes that the reason for this is the un-

E

punctuality of my company, it is my obligation to provide proof that the facts run contrary to his assumption. When the office manager supposes that one of his clerks has made a mistake, the obligation falls upon the accused clerk to provide proof that this assumption is incorrect. The office manager has neglected his duty to examine the facts before expressing his assumption. Suppositions of this kind, particularly when subsequently proved untrue, result in vexations and eventually in a mutual loss of confidence between the participants. A good discussion should not contain suppositions expressed in the form of statements.

6 "If you are interested in my ideas on this subject . . ."

It has already been indicated that a conversation cannot consist solely of a sequential arrangement of facts. The personal interest and commitment of the participants is essential. This personal commitment demands that the participant is willing and able to assess the value of facts and pieces of information and to develop his own opinion from this assessment.

An opinion never raises the claim of having general validity. An opinion is subjective and springs from the person and the personal interests which have motivated the discussion. Of course an opinion must have a basis in fact. Take the presumption in the following statement: "I am of the opinion that this year we shall have a very rainy summer. Admittedly I cannot offer any proof, but nevertheless it is my firm conviction." Here there has been an incorrect choice of words. This statement does *not* express an opinion. But if the same statement was based on a study of the general weather situation, on statistical calculations and comparisons of similar weather situations, one would then have the right to speak of an opinion.

Opinions have a dubious quality. It is tempting to regard an opinion which seems to have been confirmed by long experience as a fact in itself. One doesn't say: "It is my opinion that it must be possible to get from London to Carlisle in five hours," but: "The journey can be done in five hours." It is easy to treat an opinion disguised as an assertion as a fact for the rest of the discussion. One should always aim to be clear as to where the boundary is to be drawn between fact and opinion.

7 " This must remain a matter for speculation"

This type of statement is typical of lawyers. It has its origins in legal debate. It is a type of statement very closely associated with contradiction. It is very frequently encountered in discussions as a reaction to an assertion which does not admit of any hypothetical resolution. The statement, "It can be regarded as a matter for speculation that . . ." is intended by the person using it to say that he wishes neither to confirm nor to cast doubt upon the other person's assertion. He considers the assertion to be without any great significance for the further course of the discussion or the proof of the arguments, and therefore wishes to disregard it.

A difference of opinion has arisen between two men over an incorrect delivery. One of them maintains that there was insufficient and misleading information on the order form. The other claims that the information was sufficient, and that it was the staff in the supplier's company who misinterpreted the order. In this case it is not so much a matter of who is right and who is wrong, but rather of what measures can be taken to satisfy the customer. The supplier therefore presents his argument in the following way: "Let it remain a matter of speculation where the error actually occurred. But let's see what can be done to put things right." This example illustrates how the statement technique is suitable for neutralising an impending argument.

8 "Mr. X has convinced me with his arguments!"

It has already been shown that an essential difference between a discussion and a debate is that in a discussion one wishes, with a high degree of personal commitment, to convince other people with one's arguments, while remaining open to persuasion. In the discussion it is not crucial to save face at all costs or to defend one's prestige. It is to the credit of any participant in a discussion if he allows himself to be convinced by superior arguments. In such a case he should admit it openly. The admission of having been convinced by another person not only facilitates the progress of the discussion but also makes it easier for the other person to present his ideas on other occasions and different subjects.

Just as one allows oneself to be convinced by better arguments in a discussion one should also openly admit mistakes, errors of judgement or having gone about something the wrong way. No one is infallible. Anyone who attempts to project an image of infallibility loses credibility in the eyes of other people. Statements such as: "Nothing like this would ever happen to me", "I have never yet been wrong in matters of this nature", "I simply don't see how anyone could do something like that", make a hollow and bombastic impression. The open admission of a mistake and readiness to accept responsibility for it is an attitude which always wins respect.

CHAPTER XVI

The Art of the Summary

Besides the question and the statement, the summary is of great importance in a discussion. It is important that the summary actually does summarise what has been said. The summary is objective and neutral in value. It should not be used to give prominence to one's own ideas and statements. There has been a trend recently, especially in television discussions, for the chairman or the leader of the discussion to abuse his opportunity to summarise by changing the emphasis in certain areas of the discussion and thus lower or heighten the arguments of the various participants.

Every participant in a discussion has the right to summarise sections of the discussion. It is no one person's prerogative. If anyone thinks that he can help the discussion by summarising, he should certainly do so.

1 Summaries can be used to order the discussion

A discussion which is allowed to consist solely of statements and contradictions generally yields no results. A useful method of preventing such pointless meandering is to divide the subjects under discussion into sections. In addition to the actual arranging of the material, it has to be processed mentally. The summary helps this mental processing. If I have a differing opinion on one aspect of a subject, I can indicate this by means of a summary, and by means of a pause in conversation, I can give others the opportunity to express their own attitude. This procedure helps build up a mental discipline and prevents opinions repeatedly being expressed on the same subject.

2 Summaries can be used to control the discussion

The summary is frequently used by the chairman of a discussion to maintain the "thread". This thread symbolises a straight line from the point of departure to the goal of the discussion. Both main participants must be concerned to see that this goal is reached as economically as possible, i.e. with the least expenditure of effort. Nevertheless again and again, for any number of reasons, a discussion may tend to drift in another direction. The summary provides an opportunity to bring it back on course. Making a summary of the entire content of the discussion up to that point is more effective for promoting contact than such bald statements as: "I think we ought to get back to the subject", or "I don't think that has anything to do with the subject".

Finally, the "arranging" and "controlling" effects of a summary can be combined. Assume that one of the participants in a discussion has expressed a number of interesting ideas on a certain subject. He himself or even the other main participant can arrange the ideas which have been expressed in a summary, at the same time suggesting how they are to be discussed, what he considers should have priority and perhaps which subjects could be discarded.

3 Summaries can be used to express ideas in concrete form

It may become evident in the course of a discussion that one of the participants has to give a lengthy explanation. Perhaps he has to describe a certain object, explain a procedure, deliver a short report or something of this nature. It would be much easier for the other participants to follow the explanation if a short summary consisting of a few sentences is given at appropriate points. A short summary should also be given at the end of the description to enable the listeners to ask questions or make their own comments on what they have heard. A summary of this type does not need to be a repetition of the entire talk. Its purpose is to bring to the attention of the listeners once again those points in the talk which the speaker considers to be of particular importance.

The summary has a key role to play in the "appraisal" style of discussion. To refresh our memory: the appraisal style is intended to guide the listener mentally towards the conclusion, i.e. the desired outcome of the talks. It is therefore expedient, before carrying the arguments any further, to summarise what has gone before and then to proceed with further specific statements on the basis of this summary. This makes it easier to refer back to the last mutually agreed statement, should any contradictions be expressed.

4 Summaries can be used to make a discussion more objective

The summary is an exceptionally helpful means of making a discussion more objective. Dangers are always associated with discussions in which emotions are involved to a greater extent than reason. The main types of statement in emotive discussions are the opinion and the supposition. Using these forms of statement it is possible to pursue a conviction to the point of blindness. The summary is extremely useful as an aid in resolving such confining situations. It enables one first of all to thrash out what is fact and what is opinion. It can also be used to reduce opinions to the facts from which they are derived, so that the discussion is made more objective.

5 Summaries can be used to bring a discussion to its conclusion

Most people experience more difficulty in finishing than starting a conversation. Quite often one seems to be in the middle of a conversation, yet feeling that every point that could possibly be raised has already been discussed. The conversation drags on painfully for a while because neither of the participants can find an opportune point at which to terminate it. Neither of them is familiar with the technique of concluding a discussion. One somehow feels that a discussion which has essentially been useful and satisfactory for both parties should not be discontinued abruptly. The summary can be used to initiate the final phase of the discussion. In principle it is the prerogative of the host to conclude a discussion. The guest may only seize the initiative and conclude the discussion of his own accord if the host expressly or tacitly declines to exercise this right.

The concluding summary should not be a brief lecture on the entire discussion delivered from the speaker's point of view. It should emphasise whatever areas of this discussion appear important to him. The summary should lead into a statement as to possible consequences of the discussion.

The termination of the discussion can be supported by clearing up files and documents used in the discussion, or gestures expressing the idea of summary and conclusion. Special problems connected with concluding a discussion will be dealt with later.

CHAPTER XVII

Digression: "May I make a few notes?"

In seminars and exercises in conversational technique I am repeatedly asked whether it is bad form for individual participants to take notes during a discussion. In principle there are no objections to this practice. On the contrary, difficult discussions in which information is exchanged or in which commercial agreements are discussed or even concluded, must be accompanied by notes. However, frankness must prevail between the various participants at least on points such as: What can be regarded as suitable for noting down and what should be avoided? What is the purpose of these notes? With what degree of confidentiality should the notes be treated outside the negotiations? Should they remain confidential up to a certain stage in the discussion?

Everyone taking part in the negotiations should be clear as to whether notes are being taken or not. It is bad practice if one of the participants, without forewarning the others, suddenly begins to take notes or even, as I myself once witnessed, if one of the participants takes out a block of printed questionnaires, and during the discussion attempts to fill in the answers to the questions using symbols, reference numbers or code words. The correct procedure is to ask the other person whether he has any objections to notes being taken.

This request can be presented as a compliment to the other party. He has been giving me such interesting information that I want to make sure that I have not forgotten anything. In order to demonstrate to him once again that all one has written down in the form of notes has been the information he has given, it is a good idea to read out the notes either at the end of the discussion, or if notes have only been taken during part of the talks, when that part of the talk is over: "Let me just read you the notes I have taken. I would be grateful if you would tell me whether I have got everything down correctly."

The host can remove all doubt from the matter of making notes during the discussion by placing writing materials at the disposal of the other participants wherever they are expected to sit. Whenever writing materials are provided in this way, it can be assumed that the host anticipates that his guests will wish to take notes. The guests may then exercise this right without further ado.

Of course, participants in a discussion may request that unofficial statements or information should not be recorded in writing. Clients discussing commercial plans, future investments and similar matters often make such a request: "Please do not put anything I say during this discussion in your records. I don't know how this whole affair will turn out, and I would not want this discussion to influence other talks unduly.

In this situation one definitely should not take any notes, no matter how interesting the discussion may be. It is both tactless and a gross breach of confidence to take notes secretly on a desk pad or one one's shirt cuffs.

Not only is the fact that notes are taken important for the participants in a discussion, but also the question of what they are intended for. Negotiators often give each other assurances that "whatever is said here will not go beyond these four walls". Yet hardly is the discussion finished than a detailed set of minutes is drawn up, containing all the other person's statements, and distributed widely throughout the company. The note at the head of such a memorandum, stating that the information is "confidential", is ludicrous in the light of the casual treatment given to so-called "confidential" matters.

Statements such as: "I will not discuss the content of this discussion in my company" lack credibility from the start. Anyone who takes part in business discussions knows that in every firm there exist obligations regarding the passing on of information at all appropriate levels. The above statement would – taken seriously – represent an act of disloyalty towards one's own company. No employee would act with disloyalty towards his superior or his colleagues for the sake of the man he is negotiating with, and with whom he has no such direct relationship. Every participant in a discussion can express his own wishes as regards the circle of people who are to be informed about the content of the talks. The other parties must then consider whether they can comply with his wishes or whether this would result in a conflict of conscience. If confidentiality and restricted access to the information contained in the minutes has been agreed upon for a certain number of people, this circle can only be extended on the basis of mutual agreement. No participant has the right to extend it to privileged persons of his own accord, even if these people have also given a pledge of secrecy.

Finally all participants in a discussion should be clear as to the significance to be attributed to notes. Negotiations on a sales contract, especially in the case of large-scale projects, often extend over weeks and months and culminate in a contract which as a rule consists of the general business conditions of the parties involved as well as a number of legally relevant facts. On conclusion of the contract have all the discussions, all the questions and answers, all the assurances and wishes which have been expressed or given, automatically become irrelevant? May they be referred to afterwards for interpretation of the contract? A good illustration of this is provided by the minutes of the treaties concluded between various East European countries and West Germany during the early 1970's. Although both parties in each negotiation declared that all questions had been finally resolved in the text of the agreement and that the agreement could only be interpreted on the basis of the actual text, the Federal German Opposition insisted that the notes which were made during the negotiations provided important indications as to the significance and intention behind certain expressions to be found in the text of the agreement.

Let us leave the political arena and return to the commercial sphere. Contracts frequently contain a clause to the effect that all relevant matters in the contract have been expressly and finally settled. Supplementary agreements which are reached outside the contract must be drawn up in the same form as the contract itself. In spite of this clause it would be naïve to assume that the discussions and statements made by the parties involved would be without significance for interpreting the contracts. The negotiating parties would do well to agree among themselves as to whether and to what extent discussion notes can be used for clarification and interpretation of contractual texts. In such cases it would be preferable to take official minutes instead of mere notes – this of course with the agreement of both parties (more of this later).

Not only does the preparation and use of discussion notes frequently cause confusion, but so also does the transfer of documents between the parties. A distinction must be drawn between documents which participants exchange officially as representatives of their company, for instance prospectuses, drawings, calculations, operating instructions, reference lists, etc., on the one hand, and on the other hand, papers exchanged by negotiators for their personal information and to make the discussion easier, such as copies of letters, photocopies of printed articles, statistics, graphs, etc., which one of the participants has had prepared to speed up the progress of the talks.

If, as a representative of my company, I hand certain documents to a participant from another firm, my company is identified with these documents. My company is also prepared if need be to stand by the information contained in these papers. However, if in the course of the preparation for a discussion I make available material to support my own statements, this must be regarded as more personal.

If I, as a banker, am preparing for a discussion about his bank balance with one of my clients, and if I make my calculations on the basis of internal information provided by the firm – debtors and creditors, sales and percentage of capacity in use, etc., I am doing this to test the extent to which these figures conform to the guidelines for granting bank credit. The client could however draw completely different conclusions from these same figures.

I once observed a colleague conducting negotiations with a client with regard to a bank loan. In the course of these negotiations he had made calculations on the client's degree of solvency. At the request of the client my colleague placed these calculations at his disposal. When the application for an increase in credit was rejected by the bank on the grounds of insufficient solvency, the client in question wrote to the manager of the bank and explained that he had discussed the liquidity calculations drawn up by my colleague with the relevant trade association. This organisation indicated to him that his state of solvency in his particular line of business could be regarded as very good. It was therefore incomprehensible to the client why the bank should have refused an extension of credit on the grounds of his poor state of solvency.

On the basis of many years' experience in this particular field of negotiation I should like to issue an emphatic warning against exchanging internal documents of this nature. Personal documents used during a negotiation are based on specific background information. If this background changes, the implications of the information in the documents change accordingly. If in exceptional cases it is absolutely necessary to exchange documents of this kind, the significance to be attributed to the documents should be mutually agreed by all concerned. Moreover it must be clearly understood that documents intended primarily for personal use in preparing for negotiation do not express any obligations or commitments on the part of the company and also that they cannot be used at a later date to place misconstructions on past conversations.

CHAPTER XVIII

Every discussion has pitfalls

The impression may have been given that a discussion, well prepared and conducted in accordance with all the recommended rules, should always end in friendship and harmony. This is by no means the case. On the contrary: there is hardly any discussion which does not have certain pitfalls. A discussion can be under the shadow of certain events or situations before it is even started. Perhaps a curt exchange of letters has taken place between the participants or the companies which they represent. There may be tensions originating in the different social backgrounds of the participants. Or the subject under discussion is "hot". Perhaps one of the participants commits a *faux pas* which intensifies the heat. Anyone wishing to conduct successful discussions must be able to deal with situations of this kind. The following examples of conversational pitfalls do not of course represent an exhaustive list; however, ways are suggested to avoid or surmount obstacles such as these.

1 How does one tackle a tricky subject?

Tricky subjects are those which both sides realise from the outset will be accompanied by difficulties, arising from the motive, context or even the subject of the discussion. Basic methods of procedure are the same in every case. The important thing is to prepare exceptionally thoroughly. Be absolutely clear about your scope. What do you intend to achieve and what do you wish to avoid? You don't necessarily have to tell the other person about the latter. Your aim should be to get through or past the subjects you wish to avoid as fast as possible, and to guide the discussion in the most desirable direction.

Whatever has happened belongs to the past and cannot be changed. If you've made an error, apologise for it but leave it there. Giving lengthy explanations of why such and such happened in such a way and how the mistake arose makes the person concerned more conscious of the mistake. The objective aim of the discussion is not: "How did this mistake arise?" but rather: "Are there possibilities for future co-operation in spite of this error?" Should the mistake be mentioned again, do not attempt to minimise its importance. It is not a trifling matter for the person affected by it, otherwise this difficult situation would not have arisen.

If one party asks the other for a discussion, then it will be clear to both that the tension existing between them will be discussed. The degree of readiness to meet can be taken as an indication of the desire to find a solution. Very few people would agree to a meeting simply to repeat their previous opinions.

If the man you are in disagreement with asks for a meeting, don't approach him as the personification of an uneasy conscience. Looks of abject misery and a tear-choked voice do not relieve any tensions or rectify any mistakes. Enter the discussion with a feeling of security due to the knowledge that even if considerable tensions exist between you, you have something to offer him. Don't approach the tricky subject solely from your own point of view, but emphasize the common ground where your interests coincide. By adopting this attitude the other person is favourably impressed. After all, it is already a point in your favour that you are prepared to admit a past error and to accept is consequences. Concentrate on interesting the other person in future co-operation.

It cannot be over-emphasized, however, that the person who has made the error cannot resolve an awkward situation by offering material concessions, e.g. better prices, higher discounts, shorter delivery periods – by attempting to buy confidence. To offer an improvement in the quotation makes the other party think: "Obviously I have been paying far too much up to now. If this row hadn't taken place, he would still have been demanding the higher prices." Annoyance, rather than readiness to make allowances, would be the consequence.

It is much more difficult to approach the other person about his own misconduct or misjudgement than to tackle a difficult situation for which one personally accepts full responsibility. I am thinking particularly of a situation in which I consider the misconduct of the other party to be very serious, although I am still interested in future co-operation with him.

Assume that I as a banker have terminated the credit of a client because of his continual violation of agreed credit levels. This client is nevertheless of great commercial value to me and therefore I do not wish to lose him. You may say surely the answer is simple. All you need to do is withdraw the cancellation of the client's credit and continue the business relationship. This, however, would be short-sighted. The main aim of the discussion must be to offer the client the possibility of continuing the business relationship by modifying his behaviour. Another aim must be to make clear to the client the advantages which would follow upon a change in his behaviour.

I must be very conscious that, when discussing the behaviour of my client, my attitude will make all the difference. If he feels that I am attempting to educate him, his reaction will be one of rejection. So I don't say: "What you have been doing in the past is wrong, and you must change", but rather: "A different way of conducting your affairs would have favourable consequences for our business relationship."

Disagreement and tensions are not always the cause of delicate situations. For various reasons certain subjects may become difficult to discuss.

Examples:

The luxury car salesman must make it clear to his customer, who is already prepared to complete the sale, that before the contract is signed the customer's credit worthiness must be investigated. The furniture salesman must persuade his customer to make a deposit when the transaction is concluded.

Automobile and furniture salesmen know from experience that matters of this nature are regarded as an imposition. They also know that some customers react very emotionally in such cases, cursing the salesman, the firm and the product itself and withdrawing their decision to buy. Nevertheless the matter must be cleared up. The only question which remains is how and when. It is certainly unwise to put it off until there is no longer any room for evasion. Difficult questions cannot be resolved with one's back to the wall.

Problems of this kind should be raised during the information phase. It has already been said that a discussion can only be conducted successfully if the participants have access to equal information. If I have access to information which may be of significance for the course of the discussion, it is my duty to draw the attention of the other party to it.

2 Contradictions have many causes

If one acts in accordance with popular conceptions of how to conduct a business discussion, there is an excellent method of transforming a discussion into a string of contradictions – the so-called "Yes, but . . ." technique. However, this is not as simple as it seems.

First it must be appreciated that a contradiction is not always a contradiction. Only when I recognise the true causes of the apparent contradiction can I adopt the correct tactic for the next move. Some time ago I witnessed the following scene in a fashion shop. A young lady stood in front of a mirror trying on an evening dress. The saleswoman assured her that the dress was a perfect fit and that the colour was an excellent match for her complexion and the colour of her hair. The young lady's face betrayed her obvious agreement with the saleswoman. She then enquired about the price. It was little short of a hundred guineas. Her expression changed instantly. Suddenly the dress was no longer an excellent fit. It was too tight, it wrinkled when she walked, the neckline was not quite right, the colour made her look far too old. She contradicted everything that was previously agreed. And why did she do so?

She said that the dress did not fit, but what she really meant was that she could not spend so much on a dress. She said that the colour was unsuitable, but really meant that for this price she could get at least five dresses three shops down the street. The contradictions were not meant to be taken seriously. They were nothing more than an attempt to withdraw from a situation in which she had overreached herself, without losing face. The saleswoman would have been ill-advised had she attempted to refute the customer's objections. In fact she did not try to do so. She reacted as one ought to react in such a situation. She allowed the customer to withdraw.

If I realise that the other party to a discussion is attempting to free himself from an awkward situation by means of unjustified contradictions, I ought to come to his assistance. One should not try to destroy his superficial arguments.

Another type of contradiction which is not really a contradiction is the "provocative" contradiction. It is a much-used conversational tactic to obtain explanations of certain matters.

A prospective tourist visits a travel agent for advice about his summer holiday. He already has certain preconceptions as to the price he is willing to pay, he wants to go where it is warm, where there is water, where he can eat well, etc. The lady at the desk suggests a trip to Morocco. This suggestion arouses the interest of our would-be traveller. He asks for more details about the country itself, the accommodation, food, possibilities of bathing, etc. However he asks for additional information not by means of questions, but through contradictions. He does not say: "Tell me something about the weather". He prefers to start off with: "Morocco is far too hot at this time of the year."

What is his purpose in coming out with this assertion? He would like the assistant to assure him that Morocco is by no means too hot during this season, that there is a cool sea breeze, that at night it is even rather cold, etc. Similarly he does not ask: "What is the food like there?" He says: "Moroccan cooking will certainly not agree with me. African cooking is far too heavy for a European." He is hoping that the assistant will assure him that African cooking is in no way too heavy and only differs from European cooking by virtue of its richness and variety.

The provocative assertion shows that in principle the advice given so far has achieved its aim. It is the concern of the person offering the advice to follow up with further facts, for she has already made an impression on the listener. Presenting new arguments is not recommended. They might even have a negative effect.

Even real contradictions can have a variety of underlying causes. There is the contradiction based on superior knowledge. One participant in a discussion expresses a contradiction because he has specialised knowledge in the sphere which is under discussion, or because he has access to more recent information than the other person. In such situations it would be absolutely incorrect to contest his statements. Only one type of reaction is possible: acknowledge his superior knowledge and encourage him, by means of follow-up questions, to impart this knowledge. Recognition raises the status of both parties, even the person making the concession.

The most common cause of contradiction is the misunderstanding. Someone expresses a contradiction either because he has completely failed to understand the arguments of the other person, or because certain ideas or statements yield conflicting interpretations due to different background information. Contradiction arising from misunderstanding is evident when the significance of certain facts is not given due attention. It cannot be removed simply by repeating the same arguments once more, possibly in a louder voice. Either one must attempt to repeat the same arguments in a different way or one must advance new arguments.

This latter point illustrates an important principle of negotiating technique: do not put all the arguments supporting your statements in a long list at the start of your talk. The talk should be begun with powerful arguments intended to arouse the interest of the listener. However, a few arguments of equal weight should always be retained for use in difficult situations – such as the contradiction arising from misunderstanding – which might occur later in the discussion. The stereotype repetition of arguments in the face of a contradiction wearies the other person and gives the impression that the person speaking has nothing new to say. One is constantly coming across mediocre salesmen who have learnt a few arguments by heart. They repeat the same things again and again; the effect is one of great monotony because the listener is forced to ask the same questions again and again without actually learning anything new.

If the listener has misundestood the speaker's arguments and if he contradicts him for this reason, this is not his fault but the speaker's. Expressions of speech which are intended to shift the blame for the misunderstanding on to the listener are sheer impertinence. Expressions commonly used for this purpose are: "It is really not possible to put it in more simple terms." "Have I made myself sufficiently clear to you?" "Of course it is not easy to explain such difficult ideas to a layman." It is not the task of the listener to convert into his own mental terms of reference what the other person has been saying; it is the duty of the person speaking to present his knowledge so that it will be comprehensible.

Contradiction can also arise simply because of disagreement with the ideas and lines of argument which the other person is putting forward. Once again the underlying cause may be found in different background information or the differing interests of the persons concerned. In such situations the speaker should not attempt to pursue his argument. He must find out the reason for the contradiction in order to present new and effective arguments. He should revert from the argument to the information phase of the discussion by means of a question: are we basing our argument on the same information? Are we still in agreement about the aim of this discussion? What points are we agreed upon? One can only return to the presentation of proof after these fundamental questions have been cleared up. It is useless simply to repeat the arguments which have already led to the contradictions. New arguments employing techniques such as illustrations, comparisons, etc., should be adapted to the situation. One should also be careful not to be aggressive in such situations. The other person is not wrong, he is simply seeing things from another angle. His information is not at fault; but it is derived from different sources. Concepts of "wrong" and "right" cause a hardening of attitudes in a discussion. "Different" is, however, a bridge between the participants which allows for ultimate agreement.

If an agreement on the basis of common interests becomes impossible, the discussion can still be pursued on a hypothetical plane. "Let us take your arguments to start with. What would the consequences be? Then let's work on the basis of my arguments: what would the consequences be in that case?" Alternative solutions of this nature must be considered.

For the sake of completeness, one more form of contradiction must be mentioned here. Basically it is not a contradiction, but a device used merely to start an argument. Here I mean contradiction for the sake of contradiction. Its use indicates a lack of readiness to engage in discussion on the part of the person who employs it. He is looking for a confrontation, not a discussion. There is only one way to react in a case like this: try to make the other person willing to join in a proper discussion.

The rejection of the principle of discussion and the urge for confrontation must have a reason. Perhaps the other man lacks faith in your readiness to participate. The schoolboy who is called in to the headmaster because he has been up to mischief doubts that the headmaster is inclined to enter into a discussion. He tacitly accepts that the headmaster "has it in for him". As a result he becomes stubborn, says nothing at all, or disputes everything from the start and cannot be brought to discuss the subject at hand. The bank customer who is asked to report to another counter to give information about his financial position assumes right away that the bank is going to make difficulties for him. He will be preoccupied with defending himself. In every question and statement he will see an overt or covert attack and react accordingly. Behaviour such as this may be due to prejudice. Children sometimes display such an attitude towards older generations, and vice versa. Most people who drive cars exhibit a similar form of prejudice against the police.

Special techniques must be employed to reduce the aggressions which lie behind this attitude of prejudice. This is the reason for the contact phase. Contradiction for the sake of contradiction indicates that there is insufficient contact between the participants.

It is senseless to continue the discussion. One must revert to the contact phase. In an extreme case one would have to be content with nothing more than a contact talk to pave the way for further discussion at a later date. I once conducted contact talks two or three times a month for a whole year with a customer I was interested in, to free him of his prejudices. When he had been only a small business man, no banks had been interested in him. But since his company achieved world-wide importance, banks had been courting him assiduously. He was suffering from a number of complexes, but naturally one could not come straight out and tell him so. Numerous rounds of contact talks were necessary to awaken and reinforce his confidence in the banking system.

3 It takes two to make an argument

The most dangerous situation in a discussion is an argument. It is frequently impossible to make up for the damage caused by an argument. Thus it is of prime importance when conducting real discussions to avoid arguments, or, if an argument has already arisen, to neutralise it as effectively as possible.

One thing should be clear right from the start. If an argument arises it is pointless to try to establish who caused it. Nobody can create an argument on his own. The argument presupposes at the very least an inclination to argue on both sides. If one of the participants does not wish to argue, the other person can provoke as much as he likes, but no argument will result.

Another important point to consider is that an argument never flares up because of facts, but because of opinions. When it rains, one cannot argue about the current state of the weather. If the Government has just announced that last month's imports were 12 per cent higher than the previous month, one can hardly argue about whether imports have risen or fallen. Arguments are built around a confrontation of opinions and these can be wrong on both sides. If in a discussion my basic assumption is that it is only the other man who is at fault, I must not be surprised if he takes the same line about me. Whenever the prospect of an argument looms on the horizon, ask yourself: Do I want to take part in an argument? Do I understand why we are in disagreement?

An inclination towards argument can be rooted in many things, for example, uncertainty about the subject being discussed, lack of confidence in discussion technique, a feeling of inferiority, prejudice, prestige considerations, envy, etc. This list could be extended considerably. Anyone can come to terms with many of these factors when preparing for the discussion, if the desire is there. For example, I can get to know the material more thoroughly; I can improve my discussion technique; I can get to know more about the other man.

Confidence is the best weapon in preventing argument. The other person will be less inclined to argue if you radiate peacefulness and security.

When it comes to that other feature of arguments, opinions, I must consider the basis on which my opinion was formed. If it is based more on emotion and prejudgement, perhaps even on a certain intellectual arrogance, it will be more susceptible to argument that if it is based on facts. Therefore in principle I should act on the assumption that I must look for errors within myself, in order to put matters right.

Unfortunately one cannot always be such a cool calculator. One generally realises too late what one has let oneself in for. The problem is then how to get out of a difficult situation.

One must try to be objective. A discussion which did not start off as an argument must have had a common factor at some point. One should therefore have the courage to discontinue the argument and return to the last point of agreement. "Let us put aside for the moment the question of who is right about this. We were in agreement on the following points. . . ." An alternative course is to attempt to explain the basis of one's opinions. "I would suggest that before arguing further we ought to try to understand the basis of our respective views." Facts are more amenable to comparison than opinions. If the opinions are based on facts, then it will certainly emerge quickly that once again different information, different assumptions, use of different sources, etc., were responsible for the disagreement. If these differences are brought out, there is a chance of finding a satisfactory solution.

Another way of neutralising an argument is to use a simple conversational trick. As a rule, I reject the use of tricks in a discussion. If, however, it benefits both parties to the discussion, a trick may be called into play in exceptional cases. This trick consists of interrupting the discussion in order to guide the other person towards consideration of an object of mutual interest. "Excuse me for interrupting the discussion briefly, but I have just remembered something which I am sure would interest you. . . ."

A further possibility is temporarily to discard the contentious subject. "At the moment I don't think we can reach an agreement on this subject. I suggest that we give this problem further thought and came back to it in our next discussion."

Finally, in a totally bungled negotiation it is preferable to discontinue the discussion and agree upon a new date for talks rather than to engage in a full-scale argument. If an agreement is reached on a new round of talks one at least still has the door knob in one's hand. If a discussion ends in an argument, it will be necessary to start again from the beginning.

A word of caution about so-called "mediation". In diplomacy it is usual to try to bridge over difficult situations by calling upon the "good offices" of someone. In a business discussion this amounts to an admission that one does not trust oneself to overcome a difficult situation without assistance. The services of a third person should only be called upon in cases where one of the participants completely refuses to continue the discussion.

4 Lies have short legs

It is an old joke that there are three types of lie: the dirty lie, the white lie and the statistic. But one thing is certain. Deliberately incorrect statements have no place in discussions. Some people tend to confuse manoeuvring with manipulation. Instead of using special techniques to achieve their aims they overtly or covertly seek to distort facts.

Every participant in a discussion must work on the basic

supposition that facts which he maintains to be true, events which he describes, information which he offers can all be verified by the other person. But he must also be quite clear in his own mind that the use of false statements will inevitably lead to a chain of incorrect statements.

In for a penny, in for a pound – a saying particularly applicable to the banking business. Every statement has consequences. If you start a discussion with false statements, it may be necessary to continue in this vein. But no one can keep this up. Sooner or later he will be caught up in a web of untruths. It will become progressively more difficult for him to put the entire structure of lies to rights again. It will be virtually impossible to restore the confidence which is severely damaged when dishonest behaviour is exposed. Anyone who makes false statements in a discussion must be aware that these statements will not only discredit him but also discredit the firm he represents.

5 He caught me trying to put one over him

Mention has frequently been made of the rules of the game which must be observed in a discussion. But just as a good football player occasionally violates one of the rules, so a negotiator can be caught out in a similar way. Tricks of conversational technique are employed to change the aim or content of the discussion, if either of these takes an awkward turn. Bluffing is a favourite way of infringing the rules of the game. It is an attempt to disguise an assertion or an opinion as a statement of fact supportable by documentary evidence. And there are other tricks.

The phrase "conversational tactics" has not been used much up to this point. The Greek word tactic has two very different meanings. On the one hand it means a particular form of warfare. On the other hand it means a systematic, purposive method of proceding. Here of course we are using the word in its second sense. Nevertheless, the distinction is often blurred. When someone realises that he can no longer succeed with his arguments, he may resort to "foul play".

The discussion, just as the sports arena, offers various means of dealing with a foul. The most elegant solution is the one in which the foul is not mentioned. The listener recognises that the speaker has strayed from the path of virtue. He helps him to find his way back to the straight and narrow. This can be achieved by means of a summary. Another possibility is to refer back to the last mutually agreed interim result and from there develop a new train of thought.

If one decides to comment on the other person's "unfair practice", the tone one adopts is extremely important. For instance, don't say: "You are trying to twist my words". Rather say: "You have given my words a different meaning from what I intended." By the same token don't say: "Don't try to change the subject", but something like: "I would like to refer back to the starting-point of our discussion. We had agreed upon the following objectives. . ." In this way it is clear that the other person's attempt to by-pass the rules of the game has been noticed. But in spite of this he is being offered a chance to be constructive.

Although the temptation is often very great, one should always avoid responding to a foul with another foul of one's own. This is simply a short cut to an argument. Any attempt at revenge only discourages the other person from reverting to legitimate discussion tactics. He receives moral support from the behaviour of the other side. "If someone tries to put one over on me, he deserves all that is coming to him."

What am I supposed to do if the other party catches me trying to perpetrate a foul? There is only one possible reaction: own up! Frankness has a disarming effect. If it is possible to make such an admission accompanied by a little joke, it will be a great help in ironing out a difficult situation. Laughter always removes tension. But should one attempt to gloss over or even to justify one's bad behaviour, an argument will not be far off.

One of the worst fouls which can be perpetrated in a discussion is irony. This is the attempt to use sarcasm to say the opposite of what one means. The office manager is handed a completely muddled piece of work and says "This is a wonderful piece of work, typical of Harrison". The buyer who invites a salesman for a discussion about a complaint and starts with the words: "What

you palmed off on us is the best thing I have seen for a long while."
These two small examples illustrate the point: irony is always an
expression of power. The stronger person underlines his superior
position by expressing himself in ironical terms. The person in the
weaker position simply has to swallow it. He cannot reply. All he
can do is wait for the next blow to fall.

Irony is no way of stimulating a discussion. It is in contradiction
to the spirit of co-operation. Ironical remarks of any kind should
be avoided in discussion.

Finally, the repertoire of unfair tactics includes "pointed
remarks". In order to gain a temporary advantage one mentions
matters which are unpleasant for the other person but which have
nothing to do with the matter at hand. Pointed remarks are
intended to cause the other person embarrassment, to make him
unsure of himself, and cause him to retreat into a defensive
position. Pointed remarks are irreconcilable with the spirit of
co-operation.

Not to be confused with pointed and ironical remarks are small
jokes which can be used to create a relaxed atmosphere. Business
discussions do not have to be conducted from start to finish in
deadly earnest. Small, well-meant jibes between close acquaintances are completely acceptable. It should be remembered,
however, that the effect of such small aids to communication
depends on the situation and on the people involved. A remark
which may cause liberating laughter in one situation can cause
embarrassment in a different situation. What Mr. Adams regards
as a joke, Mr. White takes to be a verbal insult. Regional differences
in attitude are important here.

Two principles must be observed with regard to jokes. First,
anyone who can't take a joke shouldn't make a joke. Second,
a joke must be the exception and not the rule in a discussion.
There are certain types of people who attempt to block any serious
thought by turning it into a joke. It always seems as if they are
doing so on purpose to undermine the discussion. And it is hard
to believe that *everything* being discussed is amusing.

6 Well, one thing leads to another. . . .

Do you recognise this situation? You have an appointment with a business friend. You enter the discussion well prepared. At first everything goes well. Suddenly, a particular word or thought is expressed which sparks off a sequence of ideas in the other person's mind. The conversation takes off in leaps and bounds. Before you know where you are, both the subject and the aim of the discussion have been completely forgotten. The whole thing becomes a conversation for its own sake. This is known as an "apropos" conversation, since each inconsequential jump from one thought to the next is introduced by the word "apropos".

You have just been explaining the advantages of your new equipment and that the Smythewell Company has already expressed their satisfaction with it. At this point the discussion starts to go off at a tangent: "Apropos of Smythewell! That wouldn't be the Smythewell who married one of the Chumley women? Apropos of marriage! Yesterday one of the best secretaries in my department came to me and said she wants to get married on the first of August. Apropos of the first of August! Did you know that Horsefield has given notice to Cowpat for the first of August? You know Horsefield, that's the tall thin fellow. And talking of thin people. During my holidays I met a fellow . . ." and so it goes on.

The prospects of salvaging anything from a conversation of this kind are relatively slender. It would be more to the point to ask how the situation arose and what measures can be taken to avoid it.

When a conversation starts to digress, there are three most likely causes. Either the ultimate aim of the discussion has not been made clear, or the digressing participant has not prepared himself adequately and is attempting to evade specific points, or concentration is beginning to flag. Once this has happened it is difficult to bring the discussion back to the real issues again, unless the interests of both parties are identical. If they are not, one of the participants in response to the other's attempt to revert to the aim of the discussion, might reply: "That may be your idea of this discussion, but I see it quite differently."

If the digression is the result of slackening concentration, nothing much can be done about it. Recognition that one has overestimated the other person's capacity for concentration comes too late. Any attempt to force the discussion will only mean that the next opportunity for digression will be seized upon even more eagerly.

It is hardly possible to compensate for inadequate preparation once a discussion is under way. One of the participants is digressing because from the outset he has not felt able to cope with the content or the subject. He has noticed in the course of the discussion that his opposite number is far better prepared or is better informed, or is capable of applying more sophisticated conversational techniques.

In all three cases it is best to stop the discussion. Whether one immediately attempts to bring the discussion to a close, or whether one continues the conversation on a more trivial level simply to maintain contact, is a question of tact. One should pave the way for the next discussion which one may have to conduct with the same person. So it is necessary to try to establish a point of reference for this next round of talks.

CHAPTER XIX

The final contact

It is more difficult to conclude a discussion at the correct point than to begin a discussion. The conclusion of a discussion should be the climax. In diplomacy the signing of an agreement with a flourish represents the culmination of a long series of negotiations. The sales contract similarly represents the final stage in a succession of sales negotiations. The credit extension granted by the banker is the fulfilment of all the discussions leading up to it. Just as in music the final chord should, as it were, collect together all the emotions of the listener throughout the work, so the conclusion performs the function of the final chord in a discussion.

The final contact has also, however, another function. It has been said that the function of contact at the beginning of a discussion is to bring the various participants on to the same wavelength and help them to recognise the real purpose of the discussion. The function of the concluding contact is to resolve the tensions of the discussion, to make the transition plane of thought easier for the other participant and to ensure that he retains a pleasant memory of the discussion whatever the outcome.

There is a difference between the final contact and the summary which concludes the discussion. The summary introduces the end of the main negotiation; the final contact is a matter of conversational atmosphere. A discussion must begin and end on a positive note. Just as the initial contact phase must provide a continuous transition into the specialised areas of the discussion, so the final contact phase must develop naturally from the discussion which is drawing to a close. An abrupt discontinuation of the main discussion and a hasty move into the final contact phase can have a disruptive effect.

If the main negotiation has proved satisfactory for both parties, there is generally no difficulty in finding suitable material for the final contact phase. In a discussion which has shown positive results, one can resort to personal subjects in the final contact phase, or the results of the discussion may provide suitable points of reference for the final contact. Prospects for future discussions or other forms of collaboration could serve to strengthen the contact.

It is much more difficult to conclude a discussion on a positive note if the main negotiation has proved unsatisfactory for one or both of the participants: the intended transaction has not been effected; no common agreement has been reached with regard to the complaint; the desired extension of credit has not been granted; the discussion has so far not given any indications of future collaboration; the company management is upholding its decision to dissolve the business relationship. In this case, perhaps one should say particularly in this case, it is necessary to take steps towards re-establishing contact. Every discussion must yield some result. We have not been able to reach an agreement on the matter at hand, but both of us recognise that each of us is committed to a certain point of view and that the subject has been discussed fairly and decently. Respect for the opponent's attitude should not be confused with ingratiation. "I would certainly not reproach you for having to do such a shady piece of business for your company. . . ."; "I certainly admit that you have done everything you can to save the situation. In fact, I will submit a report to that effect when I return to my company. After all, it is not your fault if your management has such poor judgement." Remarks such as these do not represent any kind of tribute to the other party, but are a rather clumsy attempt to drive a wedge between him and the cause he is representing.

Even in difficult situations the final contact phase should leave open the possibility of a new discussion on a different subject or with a different purpose. Hence it must be made quite clear that the negative results will in no way prejudice future discussions. One can never know whether and in what circumstances one might be facing this same person again some day. Even a simple expression of interest in him can serve to maintain contact at the end of a negative discussion. "Naturally, I shall continue to be interested in your products"; "If you have any new products which might be of interest I would be very glad if you would let me know." In popular terms, one must at least leave the other person with the certainty that you would feel able to give him the time of day should you meet each other on the street.

CHAPTER XX

Digression: The question of minutes

In almost all business discussions the question arises: should one take minutes? This is a different matter from taking notes, which has already been covered. A distinction must be made between the two different types of minutes: those drawn up by one of the participants, intended for internal information purposes, and those drawn up jointly by the negotiators to serve as a record of the discussion.

Minutes should contain at least the following information:

1 The description "Minutes"
2 The subject of the discussion
3 Place and time of the discussion
4 The participants in the discussion (In the case of discussions with several participants, the chairman or whoever is taking the minutes should be named)
5 A complete record of what has been discussed
6 The date on which the minutes were drawn up
7 A signature

As regards content, there are considerable differences between minutes which are drawn up by one of the participants for internal use and minutes which are compiled jointly by the participants. Minutes drawn up by one of the participants for internal purposes are meant to inform company employees who were not themselves present at the discussion about those things which the person who took part considers important for them to know. The discussion is described subjectively, from the point of view of a single person. This is not to imply that he is trying to manipulate the discussion in any way. However, the personal sense of commitment with which one enters into a discussion must necessarily result in an attempt at evaluation when one is describing it. The result is unlikely to be completely objective.

Minutes which are compiled jointly by the main participants are meant to provide a record of the discussion. Each participant will therefore be interested in compiling minutes which both sides can use as a starting point for further negotiations.

It is more important to know what has been achieved than how it was achieved. But there can be situations in which one or other of the participants regards it as important to know what has been said by each side on some particular point. A record of results does not exclude the possibility that, at the request of one participant, entire sections of the discussion might be taken down verbatim. Possibly the engagement of one or other of the participants in the discussion may have legal or financial consequences. In that case, it is certainly necessary to know word for word what has been said.

Who should draw up the minutes and in what form? Agreement should be reached about this before the start of the discussion. If one of the participants offers to take on the task of making a draft of the minutes, he has a twofold burden. He is obliged to represent his own interests but at the same time he must put himself in the position of the other participants, so that he can represent their interests fairly. This is no easy task.

Enlisting the aid of a third person, a secretary or assistant for example, to be responsible for drawing up the minutes, can have a disturbing effect on the discussion. Whoever is taking the minutes must be able to recognise exactly what is worth noting down. In addition, he must have sufficient command of the technical matter involved to be able to deal correctly with the terminology. If it is necessary to interrupt the discussion again and again in order to tell him what to take note of and how, not only the continuity but more important the contact will suffer.

Certain technical aids may be of assistance in taking minutes. The entire discussion could be recorded on tape – with the other party's agreement – and minutes could then be drawn up from the recording. The tape and draft minutes could then be sent to the other participants, and their suggestions for changes could be taken into account, a second draft prepared, etc., etc. This procedure claims much time and effort and is too expensive for routine discussions. It can of course be used for large conferences, but otherwise it is not practicable. Moreover, another point must be taken into account. The fact that every word is being recorded on tape can put a strain on the discussion. I have known people whose very ability to think was crippled by the knowledge that a microphone was switched on.

Tape recorders and dictaphones can, however, be used in such a way that they do not disturb a discussion. Also an intermediate result which has been put on tape indicates that both partners regard a certain section of the discussion as closed and ready to be minuted. This divides the discussion into convenient sections and thus helps to accomplish the objectives more efficiently.

Joint minutes must be authorised by all the main participants in a discussion. The minutes only take on authority after they have received approval from both sides. If opinions differ on certain points when the minutes are being taken, this fact should be noted and these points cleared up in the course of later discussions.

Whenever possible a discussion should conclude with approval of the minutes.

F*

PART FOUR

Some typical discussions

In the preceding sections we have been discussing the techniques of discussion and the rules which have general validity. In the following section we shall be describing the application of these techniques to typical forms of discussion which occur most often.

CHAPTER XXI

The discussion between two participants: the dialogue

Of all the conversations which one is obliged to conduct, the dialogue is the most common: the conversation with one's wife, one's colleague, with the waiter in a restaurant, with a shop-assistant, with one's superior, with a bank clerk, with my son's teacher, with a stranger who asks the way, etc. Although all these forms of conversation have a basic similarity, no one would dispute that the advice I give to a stranger about the shortest way to the railway station is rather different from the professional advice which I impart to my superior if he has to make an important business decision. The information which I obtain from my son's teacher about his performance in school is somewhat different from the information which I request from my business colleague. The expectations of the conversation vary enormously according to the circumstances.

A dialogue is often described as a *"tête à tête"*. This is intended to say that this type of conversation is distinguished by a certain degree of intensity, one might almost say intimacy. It is this intensity which can produce extreme forms of behaviour.

Let us consider a conversation between a patient and his doctor or between a man seeking a divorce and his lawyer. What is said in the dialogue in these cases could not be said in any other situation. The dialogue is confidential. I can say everything I have on my mind and I am certain that the other man will have sympathy for my problems. Confidentiality means that I can rely on him to conform to certain modes of behaviour. The question of tactics doesn't arise.

The conversation which takes place when applying for a job is also usually a dialogue. But the initial situation is quite different. The applicant knows that his interviewer regards the dialogue from a completely different point of view. He expects that the interviewer will resort to certain tactics. It is his intention to use the conversation to discover the strengths and weaknesses of the applicant, which can have important consequences for the applicant. Every question and every remark is considered carefully and then answered in a "tactical" fashion. Both the interviewer and the applicant concentrate on tactics. The quality which distinguished the dialogue described in the previous paragraph is missing here – confidence in being able to express oneself freely.

Still in the sphere of staff relations, there are other situations which do involve confidentiality. It may be necessary to make an unpleasant announcement to someone. This requires complete involvement in the situation of the person concerned. The dialogue form of discussion is suited to imparting embarrassing items of information and at the same time allowing the other person to keep his self-respect.

The *tête-à-tête* has its problems. What was actually said in the conversation? Both participants evaluate the other's statements differently, according to their respective situations. How often this situation arises over staff matters! The manager says to the clerk who wants promotion: "Work for six months in the accounts department, then we'll look into the matter again". All he had intended to do was to move the clerk somewhere else inside the firm. However, the clerk interprets this remark as meaning that after the six months have elapsed he can expect to receive promotion and the salary increase for which he had applied. The salesman tells the complaining customer: "I am sure we will find a way of clearing up this matter." His purpose in saying this is to keep open the possibility of future discussions; he is not implying that the complaint was justified. However, the customer tells his boss: "The supplier has acknowledged the complaint and will remedy the damage."

Here we are not dealing with dishonest intentions or with an attempt to falsify the conversation at a later date, but rather with what a lawyer would call "dissent". Clumsy or ambiguous expressions, general ideas whose meaning varies from company to company, contribute to this lack of clarity. The sublimal desires with which one enters into a discussion can also lead to misunderstandings. The father who is very worried about his son's prospects at school will interpret the teacher's remark: "Your son is not quite the worst at mathematics" as a reassurance; while the ambitious father will take it as a challenge to improve his son's aptitude in this subject.

Finally, emotions play a larger part in a confidential conversation between two persons than when several people are present. This has both positive and negative aspects. Sympathies which exist between the participants in a discussion can help to bridge over difficult situations, whereas antipathies tend to aggravate them. In confidential conversations one can employ arguments which would not always stand up to objective analysis. However, there is another danger of which one must be aware. It is very easy to be "taken in" by the personality of the other person, or the way in which he advances "cheap" arguments or tricks. Haven't we all, at some time or other, when soberly contemplating the outcome of a discussion, ended up wondering how on earth we could have let ourselves in for something like that? Then comes the sudden realisation that it was not the argument but the charm or adroitness of the other person which determined the outcome.

With emotions there is also the danger that one of the participants may "forget himself", lose control and say things which he would never dream of saying in different circumstances. The mere fact of being alone with someone removes inhibitions and makes one less careful than normally.

Although dialogue makes up the majority of the conversations which we have to conduct, not every subject or purpose is best served by this means.

CHAPTER XXII

The discussion between several participants

While business discussions often require the participation of only two people, in full-scale negotiations it may be necessary for several people to be present. Basically the participants can be arranged in one of three ways:

(*a*) Confrontation between two groups. This situation is found whenever the complexity of the subject being negotiated makes it necessary for more than one person to represent each cause.

(*b*) Two groups confront each other, but between these groups there is a third person or group without direct relationship to either of the other two groups. This situation is encountered where the presence of experts is necessary.

(*c*) Several people discuss a certain matter together, without any particular group formation, in order to find a common solution. This arrangement is usually found in committees and teams.

The conversational techniques used depend on the initial situation.

1 Will sheer numbers really win the day?

A banker friend of mine once told me about the following case. He had been trying for some time to establish contact with a potential client he regarded as very interesting. Due to the nature of this client's business, the head of the branch of this credit company would have been able to offer considerable advantages, particularly with regard to foreign transactions. Finally he succeeded in arranging a discussion with the potential client. The negotiation started in a very promising fashion. The client was interested. He also recognised the possible advantages for his business. As the discussion progressed, he brought first the head of his export department and then his chief accountant into the discussion.

When the head of the accounts department came along he received only a brief and formal greeting. The discussion was then continued from the point it had reached before the accountant joined in. The bank manager and the head of the export department happened to be discussing technical details regarding the transaction of foreign business in documentary form. The head of the accounts department, who did not understand these matters, simply sat there and was unable to follow the discussion. After listening a few minutes he asked a simple question about certain printed forms which would be needed when using the new type of account. My friend responded to this question, as he told me subsequently, with the remark: "That is a rather trivial question. Details like that can be cleared up later by the clerks. Here we are only concerned with the more important questions."

The chief accountant then fell silent until the discussion was concluded. When he was asked shortly before the end whether he needed any more information regarding the keeping of accounts, he merely said: "No". Thereupon the discussion was concluded.

My friend, who was certain that the desired business relationship would then be established, had an account number reserved and sent the firm application forms for opening an account as well as all the forms necessary for using it. For a fortnight there was no response. After this fortnight had elapsed, he rang the company and asked what the situation was as regards opening the account. The rather cool reply was that this was a matter for the accounts department. The managing director had said that in principle he had given his agreement that the account should be opened, but that the final decision rested with the chief accountant. When my friend phoned the head of the accounts department, the latter explained that after long deliberation he had decided not to open this new account. He could not see what advantages such an

F**

account would offer to his company. Moreover, he was not completely clear regarding the technicalities of using the account. He was also completely satisfied with the banking services he employed at the moment. Further attempts by my friend to induce the company to open an account, by again approaching the managing director and the head of the export department, were rejected; it was again stated that the decision regarding new banking connections was exclusively a matter for the head of the accounts department.

When I mentioned this case in a seminar on conversational techniques, one of those present said to me: "Well, it's obvious why nothing came of the whole thing. If he is up against four people, he will be crucified. He will be defeated by sheer weight of numbers." This is something of an oversimplification. The fact that in negotiations one may suddenly find oneself confronted by a number of people is unavoidable. In most cases, however, it is made clear beforehand that several people will be taking part. But cases do arise in which it proves necessary to call in other people at some point in the discussion.

There are also situations in which you must expect to negotiate with a group. Assume that you are a salesman of construction machinery, and have been invited to have discussions with the representative of a local authority. In this instance you will negotiate with the construction committee or the finance committee or some other committee. You cannot retreat from discussions of this nature. You must simply cope.

Whenever one is facing a group of people in a discussion, the following basic principle must be observed:

Do not give anyone the cold shoulder! This unhappy feeling will be aroused either if someone is not drawn into the discussion or if a thoughtless remark is interpreted as an attempt to undermine his status as a qualified negotiator.

If a number of participants are representing the other party in the discussion from the start, ask questions to find out whether all these people are working from the same background information. If this circle includes people who are not informed about previous negotiations, certain correspondence, telephone conversations, inspections, interim results, etc., this may prove damaging to the entire discussion.

If documents are to be used in the discussion, and if it is known beforehand that several people will be representing the other side in the discussion, it is essential that separate sets of documents are compiled for each participant. The confession: "Unfortunately I have only one copy of this . . . perhaps you could get it photocopied for yourselves" is most irritating.

How do I proceed when negotiating with a group? Once I have made sure that everyone is working from the same background information, it is my duty as an individual to see that all the participants on the other side are drawn into the discussion. A common error in this respect is that one tends to address oneself to the senior member of the group. He however is not usually a specialist. The specialist is also sitting there, possibly wanting to ask a number of specific questions. But he feels disinclined to interrupt the discussion. His consequent annoyance that as a specialist he has not been fully consulted will impede future, more detailed negotiations.

If the principal negotiator brings a number of consultants with him, he wishes to demonstrate that these additional people are directly involved in the matter under discussion. I must acknowledge this fact by addressing the competent specialist in the group of my own accord when need arises.

Should it be necessary to discuss a number of specialised problems with a single member of the other group, one should always attempt to draw the others into this dialogue as far as possible by means of brief explanations. If certain questions become too specialised, they should be abstracted from the main discussion and talked over separately with the relevant member of the group. If the group with which I am negotiating consists of five people, the other four will not be very pleased if they are obliged to sit by for twenty minutes and listen to a highly specialised conversation between one of their colleagues and myself.

If additional participants are only brought into the discussion after it has started, it is in the interest of the individual who is negotiating with the group to give the new arrivals as much information as is necessary for them to follow the rest of the discussion. Even when the new arrivals are briefed by the senior negotiator or one of his colleagues as to what has been discussed up to this point, one should still ensure that this briefing will enable them to appreciate the tenor and objective of one's own argument.

Another point must also be considered. I may know the job position, authority and responsibilities of each participant within the other company, but I do not know about the informal relationships which may exist. It was this problem which proved to be the downfall of my friend the bank manager. He knew the function of the chief accountant, but he did not know that this man was something of a 'grey eminence' in the company. He happened to be the special confidant of the managing director's father. He had once brought the company through a particularly difficult period. No one in the company, not even the managing director, would have presumed to make a decision against the will of the chief accountant. Unfortunately it was this very person whom the bank manager had cold-shouldered.

An old hand at negotiation once gave me a tip: "If you are faced with a group of several people and want to know who is the informal leader, see who everyone looks towards whenever the discussion reaches a difficult phase for instance, when a decision has to be taken." I took this advice and would now like to pass it on. If such a figure can be identified among a group of several participants, try particularly hard to win him over to yourself. Not by flattery or cheap compliments, but by an honest attempt to convince him. This means no more and no less than to translate specialised problems into his terms of reference.

If I myself intend to enter negotiations accompanied by a delegation, the preparatory phase for the discussion should include a briefing of the individual members of my group as to their respective roles. Who is to speak on which subject? In what way must the arguments be adapted to each other so that, for example, a lack of co-ordination between the technical and commercial elements does not result in contradictory statements?

Recently I experienced an embarrassing situation. The matter at issue was the sale of a machine, for which the price being charged represented a hard bargain. The purchaser wanted a number of technical modifications to be carried out on the machine. In preliminary talks he had already made it clear that he would be prepared to pay a suitable price for these modifications. Since the salesman did not consider himself sufficiently versed in technical matters to discuss these modifications, he asked a colleague from the design department to be present at the final stage of the negotiations.

The problems relating to design were quickly cleared up by the technical expert. In the final discussion the salesman said: "I will be sending you a supplement to the quotation. You may rest assured that we will charge you a fair price." Whereupon the specialist from the design department interjected: "But we do not charge any additional cost for these modifications. However we solve this problem, there will be no necessity for an increase in price either from the design or construction point of view."

A situation like this should simply not arise. If several people are taking part in a discussion, it should be established from the start who is to make statements about the price, who will quote delivery dates, who will give the technical advice and who will explain customer service, delivery of spare parts, maintenance, etc.

The second question which must be clarified between a number of participants is one regarding the strength and weaknesses of the negotiating position. When and in what sequence should the various participants enter the discussion, in so far as the initiative is to be taken on one's own side? Finally, it must also be established who is to determine the overall pattern of negotiation. Even if several people of the same seniority are taking part, it must be made clear whose duty it is to co-ordinate the discussion and control its direction, also who within the group more or less decides who should enter the discussion at what point.

It is important for the team leader to control the discussion in such a way that at all times he has an overall view of what has been discussed. This sounds very simple and self-evident. However anyone who has taken part in group negotiations, particularly when a number of experts are present, will know how great the danger is of the discussion branching off into a large number of separate dialogues unconnected with each other. It is in a situation of this nature that the co-ordination of the group becomes particularly important. Not only must the leader attempt to maintain an overall view; the other members of the group must do all they can to make it easier for their leader to do so.

Where specialists among the participants have to discuss certain points it is better to abstract these discussions from the main negotiations, rather than disrupt continuity. With the agreement of the other side, the general negotiations can be broken down into experts' consultations. Subsequently all the participants should be informed of what has taken place in the sub-groups.

If the main discussion is broken down into smaller consultations in this way, the individual groups should be given clear objectives. Their discussions are not an end in themselves, but must be subordinated to and directed towards the overall objective of the main negotiations. Generally speaking they should be given a time limit. Even if the actual aim of the discussion cannot be achieved in the time which is available, the chairman of the main negotiations should be able to see how the individual discussions are progressing.

Whether the results achieved in the experts' consultations should first be discussed in one's own team and the group attitude modified accordingly, or whether there should be an immediate transition from individual discussions to the main negotiations, are questions to be decided in the light of the circumstances.

In cases where a third party is included in the discussion who is not directly concerned with the matter at hand, particular forms of behaviour must again be observed. Why have I included a third party? He is there to help the participants in the discussion to achieve the aims of the negotiations. "Helping" means that this third party has specialised knowledge or experience which is necessary to realise the aims of the talks, the other participants either not being so knowledgeable or being suspected of partiality. Take the case of a house owner who would like to install a particular type of burglar alarm in his house. He has seen what he considers to be a suitable type, although he does not understand the technicalities. He would like to find out from his architect what can be done. The architect arranges a discussion between the house owner and an expert from the manufacturing firm. The specialist gives an account of the various possibilities. Only after listening to the expert are the house owner and the architect able to discuss what structural consequences or costs would arise should this particular equipment be installed.

An automobile salesman and a customer are unable to reach agreement about the value of a used car. A motoring association inspector is asked to inspect the car and to submit a report on his findings. The customer and the dealer can only continue their negotiations after they have received this report.

The expectations which I as a participant in a discussion have of a third party are clear. They determine my attitude towards him in the discussion. I expect him to take a neutral position. I expect him to be objective. Therefore I must do everything I can to prevent doubts being cast on his objectivity. He must not be made to represent any particular attitude. Although he is free to answer questions, he must refrain from making subjective evaluations. As a participant in the negotiations I should not coerce him into giving value judgements. A third-party of this kind is unlikely to be present for the entire duration of the negotiations. After listening to his report, and perhaps asking for additional information the main discussion will be continued without him. I shall be returning later to the subject of a special form of "*conversation-à-trois*".

2 When the "Mayflower" landed in America ... (The round-table conference)

Admittedly I was not there are the time. I did not witness what went on. Nevertheless I can imagine the situation. When the ship finally arrived, everyone went ashore, glad to have solid ground under their feet once more. Then a large fire was made and everyone sat around it. Finally someone took the initiative: 'All of us have the same aim. We want to survive. I think we must consider what is to be done if we are to survive in this place." This was their first round-table conference.

The round-table conference is a discussion in which a number of people with differing backgrounds and interests, different degrees of knowledge, etc., put their heads together in order to find a solution to a problem affecting them all. The subordination of the individual will and individual desires to the common aim is a fundamental feature. The "round table" is meant to symbolise the idea of common cause. At the round table there is no top and no bottom. There are no special groups. Sitting down at the round table constitutes an acknowledgement of equality and a renunciation of privilege. This sense of community and the recognition that all those present are equal and searching for a common solution finds its expression in the democratic rules which are applied. Decisions are determined by means of a vote. In the round-table conference, the majority decides what course of action is to be taken. Majority decisions nevertheless include a recognition of other opinions, even though they may have been defeated.

The primary consequence of the democratic principle is that there is no chairman by right. A chairman is chosen from among all the participants in the conference. Even so, he does not enjoy any special position. He is as it were a leader among equals. He must exercise his duty in such a way that he represents the interests of the whole circle on whose confidence his position depends. One of his most important duties is to ensure that democratic procedures are observed.

Here I shall mention only a few of the most important of these democratic procedures. Before starting negotiations at a round table the chairman must ensure that the result of the negotiations is recorded. In other words he must see that minutes are taken. Minutes must always be made at a round-table conference. Their main purpose is to record the results, although any participant in the conference can insist that certain statements be entered verbatim. Thus a decision must be made as to who should take the minutes and whether they should record only the decisions reached or everything that takes place.

As the chairman of the discussion, the "first among equals" has other duties. It is his particular task to guide the discussion along constructive paths without influencing it unduly. Although a degree of commitment is expected of him when representing his own particular interests, he must not yield to the temptation to exploit his special role by giving prominence to his own opinions.

In a round-table conference, the discussion of rules of procedure must take precedence over the discussion of particular subjects, if the democratic character of the conference is to be maintained. Apart from this, the chairman is obliged to allow the participants to speak in the order in which they ask leave to do so. This rule also applies to the chairman himself. If he wishes to speak as a participant in the discussion, he must announce his desire to do so in the same way as everyone else. There is one case in which the participants are not completely free. If the ultimate aim of the conference has been laid down by a third party, there can be no vote about changing this objective. The members of the conference can of course decide that the chairman might suggest to the instigator of the conference that the subject under discussion be changed. However, the members of the round-table conference can only change the subject matter if they freely chose it in the first place.

Finally, it is one of the obligations of the chairman to carry out voting procedures. A request for a vote to be taken is a motion to be included in the agenda and therefore takes precedence over requests to speak on specific subjects. Apart from the exception already mentioned, a vote can be taken on any subject. A vote may even be taken as to whether further motions be included in the agenda. If there are a number of motions to be voted on with regard to one particular subject, the most all-embracing motion should be put to the vote first. The most all-embracing motion automatically includes other motions.

Abstentions should not generally be allowed when a vote is taken during a business conference. A person invited to a round-table conference is expected to offer his co-operation up to and including the point when a binding vote is taken. If as a participant in such negotiations I feel unqualified to take part in the discussion, or not competent to evaluate the question put to the vote, I am free at any time to withdraw from the conference. To take part in the discussion and then refrain from voting, however, is in

contradiction to the spirit of the conference. In a business conference a simple majority vote suffices for a motion to be accepted.
To avoid a tied vote, care should be taken at the outset to invite
an odd number of participants. The chairman's vote carries no
particular weight.

A round-table conference begins with the participants making
each other's acquaintance. It doesn't matter whether this is
effected in the form of self-introductions before the chairman is
chosen, or on the initiative of the chairman after he has been
chosen. When introducing themselves (or being introduced) to
each other, the various participants should explain briefly what it
is they are representing.

After being chosen, the chairman should open the conference
by once more outlining the subject and aim of the discussion. In
this connection it can be important to inform the other participants
as to who initiated the conference or what led up to it. In order
to discuss matters objectively, the various participants must get
some idea of each other's knowledge and attitudes. How well do
they know the subject? What can each contribute to enliven the
subsequent discussion? The points of view of the different
participants should be clarified as much as possible. If I, for
example, represent Stonebiter and Company on the Committee for
the Revision of Delivery Conditions in the Blankshine Association
of Natural Quarries, I could state my position and aims in the
following terms: "We have always been very satisfied with the
existing conditions of delivery. We have never had any difficulties
with clients. We are therefore interested in seeing that these
conditions of delivery are not changed in any way!" All the
participants will then be completely clear about where I stand.

At the conclusion of the discussion, the initial objectives should
be referred to and clarified once more. If it was the aim of the
discussion to work out suggestions, these must be decided by a
majority vote. This does not exclude the possibility of participants
in the conference who vote against the chosen suggestions submitting a minority report. If the aim of the conference was to
bring about a decision, this decision can only be reached by a
majority vote and the decision should be supported by all partici-

pants unless they expressly withdraw their support, giving explanations. Democratic principles prescribe that even those defeated in a vote must bear co-responsibility for the decision unless they openly withdraw.

With the increase in teamwork in all spheres of business life, more and more importance is being attached to the round-table conference. Anyone who embraces the principle of teamwork acknowledges its democratic basis and thus accepts the idea of collective responsibility for all actions and omissions of the team.

CHAPTER XXIII

Discussions with a predetermined object

Fundamental changes in our patterns of social behaviour which have occurred during recent years have yielded an increasing number of opportunities for discussion. Starting with the family, progressing through school, social life and finally working life, the changes which have occurred in concepts of authority have resulted in changes in interpersonal behaviour. Expressed in extreme form, command and obedience are retreating more and more in the face of discussion. There can be many reasons and starting-points for discussions. Some of them are described in the following pages.

1 Leading by discussion (Staff management)

What does "leading" mean? It may be stated in general terms that to lead means to attempt to make someone conform to certain modes of behaviour. If all the decisions within the State or within a factory or even in the family are made at the top, the only possibility of ensuring that everyone else adopts a pattern of behaviour corresponding to these central decisions is to set about enforcing obedience. As it becomes more widely recognised that differentiation of the economy and the problems peculiar to industry have rendered central decision-making impossible, new relationships arise within the company structure which are fundamentally different from the traditional relationship of command and obedience. Co-operation becomes essential. The necessity for co-operation also means the need for discussions. These must be conducted to enable decisions to be taken, to announce and justify decisions and finally to exercise control. The function of the discussion is therefore not only motivation but also control.

Discussions conducted as a preparation for a decision can either be information sessions or consultations. It is important to differentiate between information and consultation. Information is exclusively the communication of facts. It is of no consequence to the informant how the recipient makes use of the information, i.e. whether and to what extent he uses it as a basis for his decision. Consultation, however, goes one stage further. A consultation has information as a basis, but supplements it with particular wishes and ideas regarding its utilisation and application.

If I go to a car dealer and ask him what new models are on the market, he will immediately give me a description of these new models in terms of technical data. That is information. If however the car dealer should choose one particular model from among all the cars he has mentioned, and says "I consider this model to be outstanding, because it has low fuel consumption, requires little maintenance, etc.," then the information takes on the aspect of advice or consultation.

Thus in discussions on a management level a rigid distinction should be made as to whether the aim is merely to give the other person information, or to try to influence him to take a certain course of action or make a particular decision. From the point of view of the informant, information and consultation have one thing in common. It is not the task of the informant (or of the consultant) to show the other party how much he knows about a certain problem; rather he should strive to make the information at his disposal as comprehensible as possible.

A senior member of an office will view the same set of circumstances from a different perspective than his clerk; the man from the technical department will regard it differently from the salesman; the designer has a different viewpoint from the worker on the production line. The principal task of the participants in the discussion is therefore to reconcile and relate to each other the different aspects of the problem.

Hardly any decision in a company is made in a vacuum. Almost every decision, irrespective of the level at which it is made, has repercussions for other departments in the company. These consequences should be thoroughly weighed when preparing for discussions and the departments affected should be represented in the preparatory discussions. Once a decision has been made, it is the task of those responsible for it to announce and justify the decision to all departments which are affected by it. As I have seen in my own company, most employees – particularly those in higher positions – find justifying decisions the most difficult aspect of their work. The act of justifying a decision is not easily reconciled with authoritarian methods of management. To justify does not mean to apologise for a decision or to eloquently request the sympathy of those affected by it. To justify is to make the reasons behind a decision comprehensible from the points of view of the persons affected by it.

Modern business management requires control and supervision as a supplement to decentralised decision-making. This exercise of control is not a search for errors based on fundamental mistrust, but rather the search for confirmation that things are progressing as they should in the best interests of the company. If checks do reveal errors, it is important that the errors are corrected, and that all measures are taken to ensure that they are not repeated. Discussion is the means by which these basic principles of supervision are carried out.

Supervision also involves co-operation. The supervisor and his subordinate need to co-operate in correcting errors and in reducing the likelihood of their being repeated. The most important aspect of discussion between them is the approach adopted by the senior person. It is his task to investigate the causes by asking pointed questions, but at the same time he must ensure that he does not turn the discussion into a cross-examination by asking only a series of closed questions.

If an employee carries out his duties properly, this should be acknowledged from time to time in discussions with him. If the employee exceeds all expectations, if he works much harder than one would normally expect, his superior should express his approval and indicate that he has noticed and appreciates this increased efficiency.

If, however, an employee does not fulfil expectations his superior is obliged to criticise him accordingly. The underlying aim must always be to create the prerequisites for improved behaviour in future. Faulty behaviour and its cause are starting points for future improvement.

Since modern management techniques require discussions to be conducted within the company to a much greater extent than ever before, it is most important for management and employees to learn discussion techniques. A discussion conducted systematically can yield better results in ten minutes than unmethodical, ill-prepared mammoth sessions.

2 "I should like to give you a report of my visit to Company X" (Information)

Kurt Tucholsky has written a delightful story with the title "Advice for a bad speaker". The facts he has observed and condensed into one and a half pages of text are unfortunately no caricature, but correspond to the reality of how so many reports are made. Thus he writes: "Never start at the beginning, always start a bit before the beginning."

Have you ever heard a colleague giving a report on a business trip? It goes something like this: "On the 15th of January of last year I received a 'phone call from the legal adviser to Swindle & Co., Dr. Know-All. I had met Dr. Know-All at the International Congress for Experts on Street Cleaning. During the discussion in the Gala Hotel in Uptown, Dr. Know-All made some very noteworthy statements on this subject of international importance. In his telephone call he confirmed how pleased he was to have made my acquaintance and expressed his wish to meet me again at the next opportunity. We then arranged a meeting for 12 o'clock yesterday at the Hotel Freshair in Mountville. I left our offices at about 10 a.m. and arrived at the hotel shortly before 11.30. Dr. Know-All was waiting for me and greeted me on the broad, flower-bedecked stairway leading up to the hotel. He assured me once again how pleased he was to see me . . ." and so on. Nothing which has been said so far is relevant information, it is a pompous self-portrait of the informant. Unfortunately many discussions are cluttered up with this kind of self-adulation. A reporting session must always be geared to the information in which the other participant is interested. If I am unaware of what he wants to know, I should find out at the start. Once this is clear, the informant should refrain from any embellishments and concentrate exclusively on the facts.

3 "I have looked into the matter and would like to make the following suggestions" (Consultation)

At the start of my activities in banking I learnt something which has been confirmed over and over again. I had a client whose average annual income was then approximately £1,000. One day he asked to have a talk with me. He told me that he had received an inheritance of over £5,000 and that this money had been paid into his current account. He wanted me to advise him as to what he should do with the money. I asked him if he had any other assets and he replied in the negative. So I said to him: "I think the best thing would be for you to open a savings account, and depending on how long you wish to bank this money, we can pay you an attractive rate of interest." He thanked me and said he would have to discuss the matter with his wife. He promised to get in touch with me again shortly.

A few days later, instead of the client, the book-keeper came and informed me that the client in question had withdrawn his money and deposited it in a neighbouring bank. Since the manager of this other bank was a close acquaintance of mine, I called him and asked how he had managed to persuade my client to transfer his money to his bank. "I sold him shares," he replied. Infuriated, I asked how he had hit upon this idea. His answer: "Because the client wanted shares." My answer: "He didn't say anything about shares to me." His reply: "Or to me." "Well, how did you find out?" Answer: "If you had taken the trouble to talk to this man for five minutes and show a real interest in him, you would have realised that he was interested only in one thing, social prestige. He didn't want assets which brought him a high rate of interest or a lot of security, he wanted an investment that he could boast about."

One tends, particularly as a specialist, to take consultative sessions too much for granted. The specialist is convinced that he knows all the problems and has the answers at his finger tips. However, there are "no best solutions." The only best solution is the one tailored to the individual concerned. Before I offer someone advice, I must know his attitudes towards the questions about which he is consulting me. A detailed information phase should therefore precede every consultation. The specialist must find out, as far as possible, the circumstances which gave rise to the desire for a consultation. Only in this way will he be in a position to project his information and advice on to this background.

No two situations are identical. Not everyone asking advice likes to be told at the beginning of a consultation: "This presents no problems for us; this is something we deal with every day. In fact only last week Unthink & Company came to us with the same problem." It is a common human weakness to attach too great an importance to one's own problems; people like to receive confirmation of their importance from others. If I imply that a person's problems are everyday matters, he may feel slighted and misunderstood.

The information phase also provides an opportunity to pick out the most important questions from the plethora of information usually volunteered. This can then be examined thoroughly and used as a basis for advice. If a man comes to see me and wants to buy a machine from me and informs me that he has space problems, and if I have a machine to offer which is very space-saving, I will stress this point about my machine during the subsequent discussion. Without this information I might have concentrated on quite different features, perhaps the economical fuel consumption or the low maintenance costs. These other features, however, would have passed this particular client by.

One other point. The client's interests and his point of view must always be to the fore during a discussion. To continue with the machine example. If I make suggestions to the prospective client about installation of the machine, I should not say to him "It would be easier for us to install the machine at such and such a point, since then we would only need short power cables." I should rather say: "The advantage for you in installing the machines at such and such a point would be that the power supply lines would not have to be moved, so the machine could be installed without any interruption of production."

4 "What can I put you down for?" (Sales talk)

Whole libraries have been written about sales techniques. The object of this book is not to add one single suggestion for the improvement of sales techniques to the 11,731 suggestions which already exist. Nevertheless I should like to draw attention to one point relating to conversational technique. A sales talk should not simply be an attempt to persuade the customer to buy a particular brand of goods. A sales talk should offer the customer a solution to his problems. Thus the modern sales talk is principally a consultation. The conclusion of the discussion, i.e. the sale itself, should be nothing more than a confirmation to the salesman that the customer is convinced that the goods which he now intends to purchase represent the best possible solution to his problems.

A salesman should always appreciate that from the customer's point of view every purchase represents a compromise. To him there is no "best solution". There is no such thing as the most modern furniture, the most efficient electric stove, the most perfect stereo equipment; there is only the best way of reconciling what is possible with what is desirable. So beware of exaggerations and superlatives when substantiating your arguments. A realistic line of argument is far more credible.

Another important principle is not to highlight the good points of one's own product by referring to the weaknesses of competitive products. Apart from anything else, this draws the customer's attention unnecessarily to competitive products. If he brings the conversation round to competitive products, all you should do is to compare generally known facts – the sort of thing that can be found in advertisements or brochures.

5 "That is sheer impudence . . ." (The complaint)

Let us now deal with a typical problem conversation – the discussion of a complaint.

If I myself wish to lodge a complaint, special preparation is necessary. It will not be helping matters if I put myself in the wrong from the start by the way in which I present my argument. Shakespeare's words: "Methinks he doth protest too much" have a great deal of truth in them. Aggression is often used to cover up for weaknesses in one's argument.

The first stage in preparation for the discussion should be an endeavour to view the matter as objectively as possible. Then appraise the relevant facts. What is the basis of my complaint? Has there been a violation of contract? Have promised conditions not been fulfilled? Is it possible to regard these deviations as being within an understood tolerance limit? To what extent am I personally at fault? Has there been any subsequent damage of a material or non-material nature? Are any third persons affected by complaint? This succession of questions to which answers must be found leads on to others which attempt to settle the complaint. What is the best solution I could hope for and what would I accept as satisfactory? Do any agreements exist either within the contract itself or the general conditions of business, which have a bearing on the handling of complaints? Are there any possibilities of lodging a claim for compensation? How far do I feel I can take the matter? Am I prepared, if necessary, to initiate legal proceedings, or am I willing to accept a compromise?

If I am intent on driving a hard bargain and am prepared to take the matter to court, I should consult a lawyer beforehand about the chances of success. If I work out my approach systematically in this way, I will be entering the discussions about my complaint with complete confidence and will avoid major errors in my presentation of the case.

Where a complaint is being directed against me, my conduct, my product or the company I represent, there are some fundamental rules to be observed. My great disadvantage, as the passive participant in a discussion about a complaint is that, generally speaking, I am unprepared for the case presented against me. A client is on the telephone and suddenly starts cursing. My secretary announces Mr. Unwin, who requests to speak to me immediately. The company receives a registered letter from my client's legal department. It is necessary first of all to come to terms with the problem.

And now, a very simple practical tip: make a list of grounds for complaint! No, I am not joking. Note down the grounds for complaints you have received and compare them with each other. You will see that most of the complaints about your company, your duties or the products you sell can be reduced to about half a dozen central issues which constantly recur in different forms. Realising the bases for the majority of the complaints probably prevents you from being taken by surprise. Now compile a list of solutions for dealing with them. We shall return to this point later. For the moment remember that the most important thing when you are on the receiving end of a complaint is not to be taken completely unawares. The next question to consider is: how do I deal with complaints? Assume that a customer appears, fuming with rage, in your office and starts to curse and shout at the top of his voice. Let him curse. As someone once told me, no one curses for more than three minutes. Cursing relieves tension. But what is much more important for you, this string of abuse provides you with information. No one who curses and rages has control of what he is saying. He is giving you information which normally he would not have been prepared to disclose.

Much more dangerous when discussing complaints, however, is the type of person who appears before you icy and taciturn, who silently places on your desk a letter, a broken bearing, an incorrect account or something of this nature with the provocative question: "Do you realise what this means?" But let's deal first with the man who inundates you with a torrent of abuse. Don't interrupt him. Let him remain standing while he delivers his tirade. When he has burnt himself out he will be only too happy to sit down. Don't be upset even if he is extremely rude. Remember that he has lost his self-control. You will achieve nothing by reacting to something particularly offensive with the words: "I forbid you to continue these personal attacks against my company." You will only aggravate the situation. Listen attentively, by which I mean express a certain agreement with him. "I can understand how inconvenient this must be for you." "This is really most regrettable." "I know how I would feel in your place." The person speaking will then realise that he is being listened to. He will assume that you are in sympathy with his arguments, which is basically the case. He will be much more inclined to discuss the matter objectively with someone who appears to appreciate his problems.

Occasionally one becomes involved in a complaint without being in any way responsible. The customer addresses himself to me, because he happens to know me, or because I am the first person he meets, or perhaps he has been misdirected by Reception. Do not attempt to ward off the customer's excitement in this initial phase by saying: "I am not responsible for such matters", or "If I may pass you on to the person responsible for these matters. . . ." This is only adding fuel to the fire. For the client who has a complaint you are not an employee with a strictly defined sphere of duties. Rightly or wrongly he sees you as the personification of the company.

Employees in undertakings with a large customer-traffic (banks, local authorities, restaurants, etc.) often point out that complaining customers tend to become loud and objectionable when they are assured of a large audience. What is to be done in such situations? Should one attempt to appease the customer? Should one try to isolate him from the multitude and shunt him into a conference room, or should one, as a counter clerk in a bank recently recommended, simply leave the customer standing there with the comment: "Under these circumstances I refuse to talk to you at all."

There is only one answer. Let the customer curse as loudly as he likes in front of everyone. After all, why is he complaining in public? Because he wants an audience. Because he has probably invested a great deal of prestige in this scene. And if you allow yourself to be exposed openly and objectively to such a barrage of abuse, the sympathy of the bystanders will very soon be transferred from the customer to you. Things will be quite different however, if you attempt to isolate the complaining customer, perhaps by pushing him into a conference room or the manager's office. The bystanders then have the unpleasant feeling that something is being hushed up. Only when one enters the discussion phase, the purpose of which is to investigate the reproaches objectively, should one attempt to go somewhere else. A confidential discussion between two people to rectify a mistake cannot take place in public.

When the first, mainly emotional phase of the encounter is ended, one must attempt to be objective about the complaint. This cannot be done by asking the other person to repeat calmly everything he has already said, but rather by attempting, by means of a summary, to extract the main relevant points from the previous tirade. Then you move on to the information phase. Here you clear up all those questions which were discussed earlier when dealing with how to lodge a complaint. Try to see the problem from the point of view of the other person. If you have the necessary authority and consider the facts to have been cleared up, make a decision as quickly as possible. It is most important to make a decision quickly when dealing with complaints. If you do not have the authority to make a decision, or if it is necessary to clarify other facts first, work out a schedule for dealing with the complaint with the other person's approval. Then he should at least be able to leave your office with the feeling that matters have been put well in hand.

Statements made by the complaining customer should not be queried either openly or tacitly. Expressions such as: "Nothing like this has ever happened to us before." "What you have just told me is technically impossible", are uncalled for. If a particular case has really never occurred before, put it this way: "This presents us with a completely new case, with which we must now come to terms." Thus the credibility of the customer is not impaired, but you have been able to express the idea that this case is new.

It is probably of no interest to the person making the complaint as to how such a mistake occurred in a company like yours. The crucial point for him is that the mistake should be rectified and if possible, prevented from happening again. A remark such as: "I will conduct an investigation into the causes of this error, and you will be hearing again from us", is completely unsatisfactory for the other person. "I shall take all necessary measures to prevent a recurrence of this error" will make him much happier.

If one has made a mistake, one should apologise for it. This apology has nothing to do with the possible consequences of the error for the firm which is in the wrong. An apology is not an admission of guilt, but an expression of regret that this mistake should have occurred. Regret expresses human sympathy which is beyond material considerations.

If I have acknowledged a complaint, I must also ensure that it is settled. There is a tawdry rule-of-thumb sometimes applied in business to the effect that: "Unpleasant matters will sort themselves out if left alone". Of course they will sort themselves out, probably because the annoyed customer goes elsewhere.

One final comment. Have you noticed how the handling of a complaint has huge advertising potential? Imagine you have been buying from a certain shop for ten years and you have never had any difficulties or cause for complaint. The good service is taken for granted. Now you buy from another firm for the first time and immediately you have grounds for complaint. The complaint is dealt with at once in a friendly and accommodating manner. What is the result? From then on you always think of this business in terms of the quick and pleasant way they dealt with your complaint. You also tell other people, your friends and your relations, of this excellent treatment and thus, unconsciously, you advertise for this firm. In no other type of discussion are the consequences of a correct or incorrect procedure so obvious as in a discussion dealing with a complaint.

INSTEAD OF A CONCLUDING CHAPTER

Inter-personal relationships

can only be understood in relation to the prevailing social background. If this background changes, relationships are modified accordingly. If the relationships are modified, the forms of communication also change. Our modern era is characterised by a departure from authoritarian modes of thinking and acting. The principle of co-operation has replaced the principle of authority. Co-operation means discussion. The sooner one begins to practice this art – and one must practice – the greater will be the success, not only for oneself but for everyone concerned.

Subject Index